MW01290832

MINDSET MASTERY

18 Simple Ways to Program Yourself to Be More Confident, Productive, and Successful

David de las Morenas
www.HowToBeast.com

ISBN-13: 978-1537129365
ISBN-10: 1537129368

Disclaimer

All attempts have been made to verify the information in this book; however, neither the author nor the publisher assumes any responsibility for errors, omissions, or contrary interpretations of the content within.

This book is for entertainment purposes only, and so the views of the author should not be taken as expert instruction or commands. The reader is responsible for his or her own actions.

This book is not meant to be used, nor should it be used, to diagnose or treat any medical condition. For diagnosis or treatment of any medical problem, consult your own physician. I recommend consulting a doctor to assess and/or identify any health-related issues prior to making any dramatic changes to your diet and/or exercise regime.

Neither the author nor the publisher assumes any responsibility or liability on behalf of the purchaser or reader of this book.

Buyer Bonus

As a way of saying thank you for your purchase, I'm offering a FREE download that's exclusive to my book and blog readers.

It's a Confidence Hacks "Cheat Sheet" that contains 7 powerful exercises that will instantly boost your self-confidence.

Inside you will learn:

- How to instantly appear more confident and attractive to others
- A simple affirmation to rapidly boost self-esteem
- How to stop overthinking things and getting stuck in your head

...and much, much more.

Download it here:
http://www.howtobeast.com/get-confident

Dedication

This book is dedicated to all of my mentors who taught me about the power of thought. From ancient philosophers like Marcus Aurelius and Seneca to contemporary authors like Michael A. Singer and Kamal Ravikant. And to my friends and family members who supported me while I researched and wrote the book. Jimmy, Greg, Rushil, Dave, Antonio, Mom, Dad – thank you all. I'm grateful for your support.

Contents

Prologue: The Power of Mindset

"You have power over your mind - not outside events. Realize this, and you will find strength."

- Marcus Aurelius

Your Mindsets Are Your Reality

Your mindsets are the lens through which you view the world.

Your mindsets can hold you back and keep you down and depressed. Or they can lift you up and propel you forward.

They determine what you think about yourself. They determine how you relate to other people. They even determine what you think is possible to achieve in life.

Not only that but your mindsets also determine what you actually do. They can cause you to procrastinate, develop bad habits, and stay in toxic relationships. Or they can empower you to achieve your goals, build a strong, healthy body, and create fulfilling relationships that drive you forward.

In other words, your mindsets determine how you perceive everything. They determine how you act in every situation. They literally create the reality that you live in.

Good mindsets lead to high self-esteem, healthy

relationships, and career success. Poor mindsets lead to self-pity, negative attitudes towards other people, and financial struggle.

Throughout this book, we will explore the power of mindset on many different levels, but let's get started by going over a couple real-world examples to illustrate exactly how your mindsets can have a huge impact on your path in life...

Imagine you're dating a new girl and things are starting to get serious. The relationship becomes "official" and you start to see each other multiple times per week.

Now let's also imagine that you broke up with your last two girlfriends after discovering they were cheating on you and sleeping with other guys. That shit hurts. Not only does the pain stay with you for a long time, but it's also likely to affect your mindset.

Deep down you're likely to believe that all women are "backstabbing cheaters" who won't remain loyal in the long run. After all, your past experience has proven this mindset to be true.

Now, when a cute girl at your office starts coming on to you at a company party, you find yourself wrestling with whether or not you should make a move or remain loyal to your new girlfriend.

Eventually, you go for it. Your belief that all women are cheaters causes you to reason that your new girlfriend is going to cheat on you eventually anyway. And this makes it quite easy to justify hooking up with your co-worker "just this one time".

Your negative mindset just caused you to cheat on your girlfriend. It altered your view of reality and made it easy to rationalize the infidelity. Before you know it, the relationship nose-dives into the typical resentment and lack of trust that plagued your last two relationships. All because of a bad mindset.

Now let's examine another scenario where mindset actually works in your favor.

Imagine you're working a new job at a software firm. You've been working there for a few months, and you're finally getting comfortable in the office.

Just like anyone else, you have aspirations to make more money and advance your career. However, unlike your peers at the office, you just read a few business books on how to climb the corporate ladder and crush it at work.

These books advised you to focus on getting your assigned work done as quickly as possible, and then pinging your boss to see if there are any other ways you can help him. They also encouraged you to take responsibility for everything that goes wrong in the office, even if it's not your fault.

While you're hesitant to implement this advice at first, because it seems easier to just keep your head down and do your work, you decide to give it a try. After all, you have a fresh start with this new company, so you might as well go for it.

You go to work every day, implementing these ideas every chance you get. Most days you finish your work around 2 or 3 PM, and then head over to see your boss and ask what else you can do. After a few weeks, you get an idea of how you can help out and start doing some extra tasks without even being asked.

Before you know it, your boss gives you a huge raise after only a few months of working there. He calls you into his office and thanks you for making his life easier, rather than being another nagging employee.

Your choice to adopt this new mindset caused you to apply yourself at work and create massive value for your boss, rather than just trying to get by and do as little work as possible.

Both of these examples are a bit superficial, I admit. But hopefully, you can see what I'm talking about. Hopefully, you can see that adopting certain mindsets can have a huge impact on your beliefs, your actions, and your results in life.

Your mindsets dictate how you perceive everything. Almost like "The Matrix", they literally create the world that you live in. They are the difference between success and failure. They are the difference between happiness and depression. They are the difference between loving relationships and lonely isolation.

Even a poor, uneducated man can be better off than a wealthy, sophisticated man. If his mindsets are higher quality, then his day-to-day life will contain more enjoyment and less suffering.

After you finish this book, you will have learned 18 crucial mindsets you can adopt right now to start living a more confident, productive, and successful life...

But first let's tackle the obvious question: *is it even possible to change your mindsets?*

Changing Your Mindsets

Anyone can pick up this book and read it, but not everyone who reads it will see results.

The difference between the man who is able to use this book to change his life, and the man who reads this book but fails to make any changes, comes down to one small thing: *the ability to let go of your old mindsets and replace them with new ones.*

In this chapter, I'll explain exactly what it takes to successfully change your mindsets.

To put it simply, you must do two key things as you read this book:

1. Be open to accepting new ideas.

2. Take action and implement them into your life.

If you read this book but aren't really open to accepting the ideas within, then you've already failed.

Look, I get it, your current mindsets have been formed over many years. They have been formed by the many experiences that combine to make up your life. That's a lot of proof you can use to justify their validity.

But the real question is: *how well have they served you?*

I'm sure that some of them have actually served you quite well. We all have some good mindsets that propel us forward, and some bad mindsets that hold us back.

As you go through the chapters in this book, you will immediately know which mindsets you agree with, and which go against your current beliefs. These are the most important ones.

As you read about a mindset that you agree with, it will help reinforce this positive belief and keep you on the right track.

But when you read about a mindset that seems "wrong" or hard to believe, these are the ones you should pay the most attention to. Adopting these mindsets will have the biggest impact on your life. You must fight against your impulse to write them off and assume they don't apply to you.

Instead, be open to accepting their truth. Be open to recognizing that your doubt is a direct result of a negative mindset that's been holding you back. Be open to actually experimenting with them in your life, and then deciding whether or not they work for you.

And that leads me to point number two: *take action and implement them into your life*.

Reading a book alone will never create real change in your life. You have to actually put the ideas you learn into action for them to have any benefit.

For this reason, I've included actionable advice for implementing each mindset into your life. If you fail to do this, then the best-case scenario is that this book gives you a quick hit of motivation that dies out several days after you finish reading it.

The worst case scenario is that you build the habit of not taking action on new ideas that you learn. And this is probably the most dangerous habit you can have.

In fact, in this information age where you can devour eBooks, podcasts, blog posts, YouTube videos, and social media updates faster than ever before, it has become very easy to form this habit. It's become very easy to get addicted to consuming new information and ideas… without ever putting them into action and reaping their benefits.

It's called "analysis paralysis" and it has become the path of least resistance. Everyone, myself included, is guilty of doing this. However, I challenge you to avoid this pitfall as you read this book. I challenge you to actually implement these mindsets into your life. I challenge you to act on them...

Only then will you be able to replace your bad mindsets, build positive momentum, and change the lens through which you view the world. And this has the power to improve every aspect of your reality.

But before we get into the mindsets themselves, I want to take a minute to introduce myself. I want to tell you what makes me qualified to write this book, and why I'm doing it.

Who Am I to Teach You About Mindsets?

My name is David de las Morenas.

I've self-published 8 books to date, and 6 of them are Amazon #1 bestsellers. I'm also the founder of How to Beast, a fitness and self-improvement website for men. While it's not a billion dollar company by any means, I get over 150,000 visitors per month and continue to grow my audience each year.

I don't tell you these things to impress you, but rather to impress upon you the power of mindset.

Just 5 years ago I was an insecure college graduate wondering what the hell I was supposed to do next. My life had been lived on "autopilot" right up until that point, and I was carrying a lot of negative mental and emotional baggage around with me.

In other words, I had developed a number of severely limited beliefs and toxic mindsets.

I measured my success and my worth as a man on my job, my body, and my romantic relationships.

At that point in my life, I had just begun working as a software engineer for a small tech company. My newfound obsession with fitness and bodybuilding had led me to build noticeable muscle mass. And in terms of romance, well let's just say I had never dated a single girl. Mixed results, based on my shallow grading criteria.

While I was proud of my new job, and I was encouraged by the progress I was making in the gym, most of my focus landed on my lack of dating success. It may me feel like a failure on a daily basis. And it crippled my confidence in crowded social environments like bars and nightclubs.

So I began to read self-help books and listen to self-help audiobooks like a maniac. I was determined to "fix" myself. I was determined to make more money, take my body to the next level, and start meeting more women.

The thing is, I was still being driven by a variety of negative mindsets. Even though I was striving to improve myself, which is always a noble pursuit, I was still living in a mental "prison" every single day.

Whenever I entered a room, I would immediately size up every other guy and compare myself to them:

Did that cute girl come here with him? I'm sure they've had sex.

How much can he bench press? I bet I'm stronger

than him.

My mind was constantly filled with aggression, confusion, and self-deprecation. And not only was this making me feel like shit, but it was also holding me back from making progress in every area of my life.

Rather than talking to girls and trying to genuinely connect with them, I would go to bars and try weird "pick up" lines in hopes of getting a reaction and feeling "validated". Needless to say, my lack of dating success continued.

Rather than building a strong, healthy body that would not just look good, but also function well, I raced to pack on muscle as quickly as possible. And while I did gain weight and build muscle, my miserable diet led me to develop severe digestive issues I continue to deal with today (in fact, I just had surgery last week).

Rather than creating a lifestyle I enjoyed, I focused on progressing my software career and getting promotions and raises as quickly as possible. While I ascended through the ranks at my tech company, I felt bored and unfulfilled going to the office every day just to do work I despised.

Now, I don't mean to paint an entirely bleak picture here. Making mistakes is part of life. And experimenting with different techniques and approaches, especially in your twenties, always leads to personal growth and improvement...

But the right mindsets can help you side-step a lot of the pain and self-torture I subjected myself to for all those years. You can see faster results. And more importantly, you can have true inner peace... even while you're still working on yourself and striving to improve.

Since starting my own business I've connected with thousands of other guys across the globe. I've learned about their struggles and personal challenges. And the unfortunate reality is that most people continue to subject themselves to these damaging mindsets. Despite being unhappy and feeling unsatisfied, they feel physically incapable of taking action and creating change in their lives. They struggle to connect authentically with other people (in both romantic and friendly scenarios). And they continue to feel like shit and look down upon themselves every single day.

I'll share the stories of some of these men with you throughout the book, but let's get back to my story for a minute.

As I continued to work on myself, my mindsets slowly evolved. I began to believe I had the potential to start my own business, rather than having to climb the corporate ladder. I began to see women as real people I could share genuine experiences with, rather than just using them to feel good about myself. I began to focus on creating a sustainable lifestyle, rather than just worrying about my bodyfat percentage and how much weight I could lift.

Little by little, I made progress. I worked up the courage to quit my 9-5 job and started working as a personal trainer, embracing my passion for fitness. Then I started to build my own business on the side. I started to eat a diet that supported my growth in the gym, but also my energy levels and digestive health. I even started to meet and date women, coming to terms with many of my deeper insecurities and negative mindsets in the process.

But most importantly, by far, was the sense of happiness and tranquility that I found on a daily basis. This also took a long time to develop. I began to consciously audit my daily thoughts and analyze my beliefs. I continued to devour books, taking key beliefs and mindsets shifts from every piece I read. And I began to value my happiness and self-esteem far more than my income level, my muscle mass, or how many women I was dating...

Not to mention, I began to write and publish books in order to share my findings with other men (and to further ingrain them into my own head). But I've never written extensively about the power of mindset. Not until now.

Don't get me wrong: I'm still young. I still have

infinite more room for growth, development, and learning. But I truly believe I have a lot to share with you about developing empowering mindsets that drive you forward in life, while also bringing you inner peace.

And, as always, the process of researching and writing this book will help me further internalize these mindsets. This book is for me just as much as it is for you.

Anyway, I hope that story paints a clear picture of who I am and why I'm writing this book. Now let's move on. Before getting into the mindsets themselves, I want to explain how the book is structured so that you know exactly what to expect.

The 3 Key Mindsets

This book is divided into three key parts:

1. Self-awareness (mindsets relating to yourself)

2. Relationships (mindsets relating to other people)

3. Achievement (mindsets relating to your goals and aspirations)

Each of these sections contains a series of six key mindsets.

In part 1, you will learn about self-awareness. You will learn crucial mindsets for developing a realistic picture of who you are. These mindsets will help you take full responsibility for your life, build true confidence in yourself, and embrace your insecurities and weaknesses.

Without a sense of self-awareness, you will struggle to be happy with yourself and live with yourself on a daily basis. You will also struggle to connect with others and make efficient progress towards your goals.

In part 2, you will learn about relationships. You will learn crucial mindsets for building strong connections with other people. These mindsets will help you take a genuine interest in other people, avoid seeking their validation and approval, and be completely confident regardless of who you're talking to.

Humans are social creatures. If you struggle to communicate with strength and honesty, you will fail to build lasting relationships that support you and drive you forward. You will also feel lonely and isolated most of the time.

In part 3, you will learn about achievement. You will learn crucial mindsets for making your dreams and goals a reality. These mindsets will help you uncover your passions, set strong goals, and maintain consistently high levels of productivity and motivation.

Without the right mindsets towards your goals and aspirations, it's all too easy to get stuck in life. It's all too easy to paralyze yourself and prevent yourself from taking action and getting shit done. It's all too easy to follow the wrong path and create a lifestyle you aren't happy with.

As I mentioned before, learning new ideas and then taking the steps necessary to implement them into your life are the two keys to changing your mindsets. For this reason, all three of these parts contain actionable advice you should take to ensure you successfully internalize each of the mindsets we'll cover.

On top of that, I've included a variety of anecdotes (from my life and the lives of others) as well as scientific studies to give you further proof and encouragement for making these changes in your own life.

Now it's time to get our hands dirty and dive into part 1: self-awareness. Let's do it!

Part I: Self-Awareness

"I know that I am intelligent, because I know that I know nothing."

- Socrates

Pain

What is the most painful situation you've ever endured?

Of all the horror, pain, and suffering caused by Hitler's rise to power in Nazi Germany, there's one story that sticks with me the most – the story of Viktor Emil Frankl.

Viktor was born into a Jewish family in Vienna in 1905. As he grew up and went through school, he developed a passion for psychology. This led him to study neurology at the University of Vienna, with a concentration in depression and suicide.

After graduating, Frankl immediately began to help people overcome these painful issues, first by offering a free program to help suicidal high school students. The program was a huge success: not a single student from Vienna committed suicide in 1931.

Next, he completed his residency at the Steinhof Psychiatric Hospital in Vienna, where he helped treat over 30,000 women who had suicidal tendencies.

However, in 1938 Nazi Germany took over Austria and Hitler began to impose his will. At first, this simply meant that Frankl was not allowed to treat Aryan patients due to his Jewish heritage. But things would quick take a turn for the worse...

In 1942 Frankl, along with his wife and his parents, was deported to the Nazi Theresienstadt Ghetto where Frankl was forced to work as a general practitioner in the medical clinic. While his freedom was completely taken from him, he managed to avoid the all-out torture of the Nazi concentration camps.

However, in 1944 the tides turned yet again. His parents died and he was sent to the infamous Auschwitz Concentration Camp to work as a slave laborer, along with his wife. When he arrived, all of his possessions were taken from him and destroyed, including the manuscript of a book he working on.

As he witnessed unimaginable atrocities day-after-day, he began to reconstruct his book. While his fellow slave laborers were being gassed to death, starved to death, and treated like animals, he observed how different people reacted to these extreme circumstances.

During this time, Frankl had some eye-opening realizations about humans and our profound capabilities to deal with pain and suffering. Although the majority of people gave in to their harsh reality, eventually dying or drowning in their misery, there were some who rose above it. There were some who continued to find enjoyment in life and who continued to display compassion to others. In his book, Frankl recalls some who went as far as giving away their only food for the day – a small piece of bread – to comfort the other prisoners.

Frankl concludes that the type of prisoner one becomes depends on an inner decision, not on environmental conditions alone. He suggests that an ultimate human freedom exists, even in the most deprived conditions: the freedom to choose one's attitude towards suffering.

He credits this realization for his survival. You see, he decided that he would survive the concentration camps in order to publish his book and spread his message. And he did. He survived and published his bestselling book: *Man's Search for Meaning*. And he went on to live a full life, dying at the old age of 92 in 1997. [1]

As the great Friedrich Nietzsche once said: *"He who has a why to live for can bear with almost any how."*

Mindset #1: My suffering is merely a test, it is merely a chance to practice my virtues.

I assume that you are not a victim of genocide like Viktor Frankl was. However, this mindset is still extremely important for you to adopt and internalize.

We all experience suffering in our day-to-day lives. We get fired, get dumped, get sick, and go through a lot of other BS that causes us pain. How we deal with this pain directly determines how happy, productive, and successful we are in life.

Frankl noted that the concentration camp prisoners who found meaning in their suffering were more likely to show compassion, be happy, and ultimately survive. And the same holds true today: people who are able to find meaning in their suffering are more likely to navigate past it, and prevent it from ruining their lives.

Let me give you a quick example from my life to illustrate how this applies to less extreme situations. I recently broke up with my girlfriend. Well, I'll be honest, she broke up with me.

After each of my previous two breakups, I was completely crushed. I would lie on the floor of my apartment, feel sorry for myself, and contemplate what I could have done to save the relationship... for months on end. I even continued to text my exes and keep hoping that we could somehow work things out, get back together, and live happily ever after.

This is all normal, of course, but it prevented me from letting go and moving on with my life. It prevented me from enjoying my life. It prevented me from growing my business. It prevented me from enjoying the time I spent with my friends. It prevented me from being truly open to meeting other girls.

This time, I adopted Mr. Frankl's mindset. I decided that I would take this breakup as a chance to practice letting go. Letting go is such an important skill to have, because when you struggle to let go, you sabotage yourself. Maybe you stay in a toxic relationship that should have ended long ago because you're afraid of being alone. Or maybe you stay in a shitty job that you hate because you're afraid of finding a new job. You paralyze yourself and undermine your best interests.

So I decided to view this recent breakup as a test of my ability to let go. And you know what? I've bounced back faster than ever. Sure, I still cried, felt sorry for myself, and wondered what could have been. Some degree of suffering is inevitable. But I side-stepped the pitfall of dragging this period out for months on end.

The amazing thing is that you can use this mindset to overcome virtually any type of suffering.

Even if you're just anxious because you haven't heard back from a potential employer after an interview – or because you haven't heard back from a girl after the first date – you can still give this "suffering" meaning. You can view it as a chance to practice being patient so that future situations like this don't stress you out as much.

Even if you're just angry because your neighbors kept waking you up last night – or because your girlfriend bailed on your plans – you can still give this "suffering" meaning. You can view it as a chance to practice forgiving other people, even if you decide to have a talk with your girlfriend – or confront your neighbors – in the process.

Give your suffering a meaning, and then watch it dissipate. Watch it drive you forward. Watch it supercharge your personal growth.

Perfection

How would you define living a perfect life?

A number of interesting studies have been conducted on the psychological side effects of chasing perfection.

But before we dive into the studies, let's define exactly what perfectionism is, so you can see how it applies to your life and affects your mindsets.

Most people believe that perfectionism only applies to the work that you do. Most people think it only applies to the papers you write, the reports you prepare, or the presentations you create.

But it also applies to YOU... as a person.

Almost all of us try to portray a perfect image to the world around us. We all have insecurities we're ashamed of. We all have things we try and hide from other people. We all want to look as good as possible when we leave our homes. We all want to be perceived as attractive, confident human beings so that other people will respect us. None of us want people to see our "ugly" side.

It's why you go to the gym and try to get ripped. It's why you pay for an expensive education, work as an unpaid intern, and then write an amazing resume in hopes of landing a prestigious job. It's why you spend so much money to buy an expensive car.

You want all of these things because of what they tell other people about who you are. You want all of these things because they make you look good. You want to portray the picture-perfect image to the world around you.

Okay, now that I've explained why we are all perfectionists, at least to a certain extent, let's look at a few interesting studies that have been done on the subject.

First comes a 1995 study published in the *International Journal of Eating Disorders* that explored the link between anorexia and perfectionism. After assessing a large group of anorexic subjects and examining multiple measures of perfectionism, the study "confirmed that underweight, malnourished patients with anorexia nervosa are perfectionistic". [2]

In case you aren't familiar, anorexia is an eating disorder that causes people to starve themselves in order to lose weight. And this study proved that perfectionism is a major cause of this mental illness. In other words, some people are so driven by their desire to have a "perfectly" thin body that they end up starving themselves.

While you may not have an eating disorder, there are likely other self-destructive behaviors you use to cope with your desire to appear perfect. We'll explore some concrete examples of how you might do this in a minute, but first, let's jump into another study.

The next study was published by the *American Psychological Association* back in 1995. This one examined the role of perfectionism in the suicides of three remarkably talented individuals. [3]

The study found that "intense perfectionism" was a large driver of depression, and that it "interfered significantly" with the ability to treat depressed patients who were also perfectionistic. In other words, not only does perfectionism lead to depression, but it also prevents you from successfully dealing with depression and improving your outlook on life.

The study even went on to suggest that perfectionism was a likely cause of these particular suicides, given that these three individuals were extreme perfectionists who experienced severe bouts of depression.

I don't mean to dwell on negative examples here, but I want to drive home the fact that striving to be perfect is an extremely dangerous thing. Not only can it lead to depression and eating disorders, it can even lead to suicide.

If you don't have an eating disorder, and you aren't prone to depression, perfectionism is still likely causing you anxiety on a day-to-day basis. You see, a final study, this one done in 1989 by the journal of *Personality and Individual Differences*, found a strong correlation between perfectionism and trait anxiety. [4]

In other words, the researchers found that people with "trait anxiety" – people who commonly experience anxiety in their lives – are also likely to be perfectionists. While this is a more general finding than the previous two studies, it's also a more relatable one.

We all experience anxiety. And it's never a good thing. It drives us to worry, feel down, and even get angry with ourselves. The fact that striving to be perfect can lead to frequent anxiety is another big reason you need to stop trying to be perfect.

Mindset #2: I am not perfect, but I love myself anyway.

As these studies have proven, striving to be perfect can lead to some pretty devastating consequences. Trying to portray a perfect image to our friends, family members, coworkers, and strangers is a very dangerous game to play. Trying to cover up all of your "flaws" can only lead to worrying, depression, and even pain.

Look, we all have things that we're ashamed of. We all have certain things that embarrass us. This is completely normal. No one is 100% perfect. The problem arises when you try and pretend like these things don't exist, or when you try and hide them from everyone you come into contact with.

Maybe you're ashamed of your appearance. Maybe you're overweight, and it makes you feel weak. Maybe you have a big nose, and it makes you feel ugly. Maybe you're short, and it makes you feel like a lesser man. Maybe you're balding, and it makes you feel impotent.

All of these things are common. They are all normal. But they are not the reason that you're feeling weak, ugly, or impotent. Your mindset is. The fact that you're ashamed of these things, and the fact that you're always focused on them, is the real reason you feel like shit.

Maybe you have sexual insecurities. Maybe you struggle with premature ejaculation, and it makes you feel like you're unable to please women. Maybe you're a virgin, and it makes you feel inferior to other men. Maybe you have very little sexual experience, and it makes you feel unworthy of attracting women.

Again, all of these things are common. They are all normal. And again, they are not your real problem. Your real problem is that you wish you were perfect. You keep wishing that these things were not true.

And this shame is ultimately what leads to low self-esteem, and a lack of sexual confidence.

Maybe you have financial insecurities. Maybe you're ashamed of your job title, and it makes you feel like a failure. Maybe you're embarrassed about your debt, and it makes you feel like a loser. Maybe you're afraid to show other people your old, beaten up car and it makes you feel embarrassed to drive anywhere you might be recognized.

Yet again, these issues are not the problem. They are not the reason that you keep beating yourself up and feeling insecure around other people. No, it's because of your mindset. It's because you can't come to terms with the fact that you are not – and never will be – perfect.

Look, this doesn't mean you should find the closest ditch and bury yourself alive. It doesn't mean you should stop trying to improve yourself. It doesn't even mean you should avoid working on overcoming these insecurities.

No, it just means that you should accept their existence and stop trying to hide them... from yourself and from everyone else.

Now, I'm not advising you to walk around proclaiming that you're balding, or that you have erectile dysfunction, whenever you enter a room. That would be pretty strange. But I am advising you to adopt the mindset that you are not, in fact, perfect.

I'm advising you to consciously admit your insecurities to yourself. And I'm advising you to stop hiding them from other people, whenever they naturally happen to come up. Doing these two things will remove the power they have over you. It will stop them from making you feel insecure, ashamed, and unworthy.

One effective way to adopt this mindset is to look yourself in the mirror and say, "Even though _____ , I love myself".

Replace the blank space above with one of your insecurities. For example, "Even though I'm balding, I love myself." Or, "Even though I always come too quickly, I love myself." Or, "Even though I'm in debt, I love myself."

Do this now. Do this often. I do it every morning.

It will allow you to accept yourself as you are. It will allow you to start living from a place of strength and acceptance, rather than a place of shame and insecurity. It will allow you to internalize this mindset and start being proud of who you are, regardless of all your scars and secrets.

Ownership

Have you ever owned a Japanese-made car?

The most reliable car I ever owned was a 2011 Honda Civic.

Hondas are known for their sturdy Japanese craftsmanship, their fuel economy, and their reliability. And the Civic is by far their most popular car.

Back in 2012, Honda decided to update the Civic. Prior to 2012, Honda had maintained the same fundamental design for five straight years. This design was extremely popular among consumers and car critics.

Even in 2011, Honda was still earning praise for the design they initially released back in 2006. Here's what one popular magazine had to say about the 2011 Civic:

"The current-generation Honda Civic looked pretty far-out when it was first introduced, five years ago, but it turned out to be a trendsetter. Its swoopier, more arched roofline, stubbier, yet more aerodynamic front end, drawn-forward, more rakish windshield, and even its bold, two-tiered video-game-

*like instrument panel, which made other small-car
dashes look plain at the time, have since been
emulated by other automakers—serving to keep the
Civic's look very contemporary."* [5]

In other words, the 2006 Honda Civic was far ahead
of its time. It set the standard for entry-level sedans
for years to come.

So in 2012, when Honda finally decided to update
the car, everyone's expectations were sky-high.
Anything less than another revolutionary design
would be a letdown...

And the 2012 Civic was far from revolutionary.

Not only did the car fail to set the bar higher than the
2011 model, but it was widely considered an inferior
product.

Critics immediately pounced on the new design. They
condemned Honda for cutting costs and using cheap
plastics for the interior of the car. And they were
dumbfounded by how bland and weak the exterior
looked compared to previous iterations.

And consumers agreed. Sales for the Civic dropped
by a whopping 15% compared to the previous year.
And this number is understating the decrease in
sales, given that the United States car industry
actually grew by 10% as a whole during that same
year. [6]

This put Honda Motors in a state of panic. And it put a lot of pressure on their CEO, Takanobu Ito. He responded by calling for a press conference. At that press conference, he issued the following statement:

"The ultimate responsibility rests with me. We take inputs from the various markets with sincerity... and try to work out the best actions for what we have observed. Those decisions rest with me."

Rather than ignoring the problem, or placing the blame on his engineers or designers, he took full responsibility for the failure – something that's extremely rare for any car manufacturer to do. But it led to some profound results.

First, it let everyone else at Honda off the hook. It removed any potential finger-pointing that would cripple the company's ability to move forward in a unified direction and rectify the problem.

Second, it restored faith in Honda customers who were disappointed with the 2012 release. Just seeing the company step up and take the blame was a show of good faith.

Finally, it allowed the company to take action and make fast, efficient strides forward. In 2013, just one year later, Honda released a completely updated Civic. It brought back a sporty design that was sleeker than ever before, and it substantially upgraded the quality of the car's interior. [7]

All of this led to an enormous 30% increase in sales during the following year, lifting the Honda brand to a whole new level. [8]

And all of this was ultimately possible because Honda CEO Takanobu Ito took full ownership of the company's failure, rather than finger-pointing or feeling sorry for himself.

Mindset #3: My emotions, my actions, and my decisions are my responsibility and nobody else's.

Now, I know you're probably not the CEO of a huge company like Honda, but there's still a lot you can learn from Mr. Ito and his decision to take responsibility.

You see, most people have a "victim" mindset that would prevent them from being able to step up and own their failure like Mr. Ito did. Most people believe that a lot of what happens to them in life is not fully under their control. They believe that they are victims to the ups and downs of everyday life.

Most people take the mindset of "Oh poor me, why do I feel like this? Why is this happening to me? Who is going to help me get out of this?"

It's the reason you blame your loved ones for making you feel like shit, rather than taking responsibility for your own emotions and being grateful for everything you have.

It's the reason you blame politicians, or the minimum wage, for not being able to pay your bills, rather than taking responsibility for your own actions and figuring out how you can make more money.

And it's no wonder that most people adopt this mindset: it's extremely convenient. It's just easier to blame other people for your misery or lack of success. It's just easier to point the finger than it is to step up and take the burden on your own shoulders.

However, there are only negative consequences to doing so. If you can reject this urge, and instead adopt the mindset that you alone are responsible for everything in your life, you will immediately boost your self-confidence and your ability to get shit done.

Why? Because things never go according to plan.

When things go according to plan, you're always going to be happy, productive, and full of energy. But when things go wrong, that's when the power of this mindset really kicks in.

That's when you have the urge to blame someone else for whatever crap you're dealing with at the time... and giving into this urge is completely natural. It's the path of least resistance. It's what most people do, after all.

But what does it lead to?

It leads to you sit there, do nothing, and feel sorry for yourself. It leads to you get angry at other people. It leads you to procrastinate and indulge a barrage of negative thoughts and emotions.

When the 2012 Honda Civic was released and nobody bought it, Mr. Ito could have blamed his engineers, worried about his poor sales, and felt sorry for himself. But he didn't. No, instead he took the blame. And then he took quick action to rectify the situation.

His mindset caused him to do this. His mindset caused Honda to set a new path and release an amazing car the following year. It's really no wonder that he's the CEO of such a successful company. There's no doubt in my mind that this exact same mindset is what propelled him forward throughout his entire career, and got him to where he is today.

So next time you catch yourself feeling down or depressed, take full ownership for how you feel. It doesn't matter if you got sick, lost your job, or got dumped by your girlfriend. Blaming your girlfriend, your boss, or plain bad luck will only feed these negative emotions and keep you down.

Instead, you must adopt the mindset that whatever happened was actually your fault. You must accept this fact and do your best to learn from the situation...

What could you have done differently to avoid this outcome?

What will you do differently in the future to avoid a similar outcome?

Maybe you haven't been sleeping much lately, and that weakened your immune system. Maybe you haven't been the best possible employee at work, and that made you dispensable. Maybe you haven't been giving your girlfriend the space she needs, and she got sick of it.

Ultimately there's always something you could have done differently to avoid a certain outcome. Ultimately everything is your responsibility. And the best thing you can do is accept this fact, stop blaming other people, and learn your mistakes.

This will allow you to make peace with your past. This will allow you quickly move forward and learn from your mistakes. And this will also make other people respect you more and see you as a leader who's not afraid to fail.

Thought

What are you thinking right now?

Seriously, what is the little voice inside of you head saying right now?

You are constantly hearing a narrative your entire life. Your head is constantly filled with changing thoughts, emotions, and desires.

These thoughts can be good. They can help you reason through a difficult problem, and come up with an elegant solution. They can plan out your day and deconstruct complex information.

However, these thoughts can also be destructive. They can insult you and tell you that you aren't capable of doing something. They can lie to you and make up an entire story that's simply not true.

One negative "story" my little voice likes to tell me is about my business, and how "bad" things are going...

Despite continued growth over the past 3 years, my thoughts can convince me that I'm a complete and utter failure. Despite receiving emails and messages every single day from fans and customers, my thoughts can convince me that nobody cares about my work.

It usually starts when I'm finishing up a project or a book. After working hard for months on end, I start to see the light at the end of the tunnel. And then I start to worry.

"What if nobody buys my new course? What if people forget about me and stop reading my material? What if I can't find any new topics to cover after this one?"

Man, those fucking "what ifs" can kill you.

Before I know it, I'm playing out some ridiculous scenario where I publish a book that doesn't sell a single copy. Next thing you know I'm homeless and begging for money on the subway. I don't know how my mind is able to get there, but it does.

Another common negative story that my mind likes to tell me is about my ex-girlfriends.

Despite the fact that all of my past relationships didn't work out for obvious reasons, my thoughts can convince me that if I had done "just this one little thing" differently, then we never would have broken up. Despite the fact that I continue to meet and date amazing women, my thoughts can convince me that I will never meet another "good" girl who's fit to be my girlfriend.

It usually starts when I'm alone at my apartment with nothing urgent to do. Then a memory of my ex-girlfriend enters my mind. And then I start to think about all the good times we had and all the things that could have been. I lie on the floor and begin the same old routine...

"What if I just told her I loved her a bit sooner? What if I didn't get pissed off every time she changed our plans at the last minute? What if I fought harder for her at the end?"

Again, those fucking "what ifs" can kill you.

Before I know it, I'm playing out some fantasy in my head where I did one little thing differently, and then all of a sudden we're back together and living happily ever after. We have two kids, a nice home, a white-picket fence, the whole nine yards...

But no, it's too late now. Now I'm destined to be forever alone! I'm going to die single and lonely! Noooo! Save meeeee!!!

Mindset #4: Negative self-talk is normal, but engaging it only makes things worse.

Here's the thing: we all have unproductive thoughts that can cause us anxiety.

There's no way around this. Even the Dalai Lama, perhaps the most "zen" person in the entire world, has negative thoughts.

It's part of life. You simply don't get to choose exactly what thoughts pop into your head. But you do get to choose how you react to these thoughts.

You can either engage them, or you can accept their presence and then let them go. You can either wonder "what if" and try and think your way to a solution, or you can focus on something else and allow them to pass.

But remember this: in the game of negative self-talk, there's no way to "win". There's no way to take a negative thought and think about it in "just the right" way so that it makes everything better again. That's simply not how it works. When you "feed" these negative thoughts, they only grow and get more control over you.

So how do you know which thoughts are okay to engage and which thoughts you should just let go?

Simple, just ask yourself: "Is this something I need to think about right now? Will thinking about this lead anywhere good?"

If you're working on a project, planning out your day, or solving a math problem then the answer is probably yes. Thinking is useful in these cases.

But if you're worrying about an ex, thinking about how dumb your haircut looks, or convincing yourself that you aren't good enough to do something, then the answer is no... HELL NO!

Negative self-talk gets its power from you. Negative self-talk is powerless if you don't engage it. But when you do, you give it life. You "feed" it and allow it to grow inside of you. And then, before you know it, it has fully consumed you.

You were having a jolly old day, and then a silly thought popped into your head. "Maybe I'm not good enough for this girl." Or, "Why did my friend say that to me? He's an asshole." Or, "If I don't lose 20 pounds, my life is fucked."

Don't do it dude! Don't engage the negative thoughts! It's all BS!

If you do, then pretty soon you're going to convince yourself that you are, in fact, not good enough for this girl. You're going to convince yourself that you need to be angry at your friend and start a fight next time you see him. You're going to convince yourself that you can never lose weight and be happy with yourself.

Instead, here's what you must do:

- *Catch yourself engaging in negative self-talk*

- *Accept that it's happening. Tell yourself: "It's completely normal that I'm thinking this."*

- *Focus on breathing deep breaths into your belly*

- *Relax your shoulders down and release the tension*

in your neck

This is magic! This will allow you to move past the negative thoughts as quickly as possible.

This works so well because it starts by simply being aware of your negative thoughts. Then, rather than trying to pretend like everything's okay, it allows you to accept their existence and avoid fighting them off. Finally, it relaxes your body and gets you to focus on something else.

After just 10-20 seconds of focusing on your breathing, you will be home free. You will have demolished the negative mindset that was beginning to form. You can get back to living your life now.

Time

Growing up, what did you dream about accomplishing in life?

I recently saw an emotional documentary on ESPN that detailed the lives of two brothers: Michael and Marshall Carpenter. [9]

Growing up in Montana, they were always very close. And they shared the same passion: the sport of wrestling.

In high school, Michael and Marshall each won multiple Montana state titles. Marshall even set a record at his high school, winning 34 consecutive matches by "pinning" his opponents (a skillful way to end a wrestling match by grabbing your opponent's shoulders and pinning them to the ground).

They truly loved wrestling. As Michael puts it, "My dream was always to wrestle in the Big Ten... and so was my brother's." They succeeded on that dream, both being recruited by Michigan University, one of the top wrestling programs in the highly competitive Big Ten conference.

Only a few weeks into his freshman year, Marshall began struggling with injuries to his shoulder and elbow. However, these injuries would prove to be the least of his problems...

While injured, he began to play video games for hours and hours, every single day. "I would think to myself, I'll just play one game and then I'll go eat," he recalls. "It literally felt like I blacked out the rest of the day."

As he continued to dedicate more and more time to video games, he began missing practices and even avoiding his brother: "Honestly, I was mad at him," his brother Michael remembers. "It felt like I was on my own all of a sudden."

After just one year, Marshall quit the wrestling team and dropped out of college, giving up his lifelong dream so he could move back to his parents' house and play more videos games.

He began to play for 8-14 hours a day, sacrificing every other aspect of his life in the process. "I felt like that's where my life was," he says, looking back.

Even after his brother, mother, and father continued to pressure him to lay off the video games, he continued. It was how he preferred to spend his time. And nothing changed until he agreed to go to a video game addiction program in Washington. In this recently created program, patients are placed in a technology-free environment so they can completely disconnect from their bad habit.

Even though he did not initially want to go, the program ended up being a turning point in his life. Marshall has not touched a single video game since.

Looking back, he admits that he sacrificed over 5 years of his life to video games. Even worse, he says, are all the opportunities he missed out on because of his addiction: "I took all of my dreams and basically flushed them down the toilet. I'm not going to play a video game ever again."

Mindset #5: My time is my most valuable resource.

Look, I realize that you probably aren't addicted to video games. And I know this example is a bit extreme. But the fact is that most people fall victim to poor time management. Most people allow hours of their day, every single day, to basically get flushed down the toilet.

You open up your phone to reply to a text message, and next thing you know you're scrolling through Facebook for 30 minutes. Or you're working and you decide to watch "just one" video on YouTube, and next thing you know you've been watching videos for an entire hour. Or maybe you take a break to lie down for 20 minutes and rest, and next thing you know you've been napping for hours.

It doesn't matter if your vice is video games, Facebook, or Netflix. Spending time doing these types of "escapist" activities is dangerous. Do you really want to be on your deathbed, looking back at your life, only to realize that 25 or 50% of it was spent sitting there and doing nothing?

Let me make one thing clear, I don't think that video games or TV shows are evil. I don't think that you need to completely avoid them. I'm simply urging you to consciously choose how you spend your time. If you decide you want to relax tonight and enjoy a movie, then go for it. But actually relax and enjoy the damn thing, don't look at your phone and scroll through social media the entire time.

Time is your most valuable resource. Once you spend it, you cannot get it back. It is 100% non-renewable. It comes and it goes. That's it! It doesn't come back again.

You must make this mindset shift. You must begin to value your time above all else. It's truly the most important thing you have.

Without money, you might have to live in uncomfortable conditions and experience frequent bouts of hunger. Without friends, you might be lonely and lack support and love in your life. But without time, you are dead. Without time, there is no you.

So man up and start paying attention to how you spend your time. If you don't, you risk ending up like our friend Marshall Carpenter. You don't have to play video games for 12 hours a day to make this mistake. Simply by wasting a few hours here and there, you are robbing yourself of precious time.

You're taking the time you could be spending to pursue your dreams, and flushing it down the toilet. You're taking the time you could be using to build a business, see your friends, or enjoy a hobby you love, and wasting it away staring at a screen or sleeping in until noon.

The extra 2 hours of sleep you got could have been spent working out at the gym, writing a book, or talking with a loved one. The extra 2 hours you spent looking at your phone could have been spent learning a new skill, going for a run, or applying for a new job.

But you won't get that time back. It's already been spent. And there's no receipt you can use to return it.

Instead, you must shift your mindset going forward. You must respect your time above all else. You must spend it doing things you love to do, seeing people you love to see, or working towards things you would love to achieve.

In fact, I would advise you, right now, to think about how you tend to waste time. Think about what time of the day you tend to engage in pointless phone-scrolling or Netflix-binging. Then think about how you could better spend that time.

Cutting out these large periods of wasted time and replacing them with meaningful activities that you actually enjoy can drastically improve your productivity and your happiness.

Now is the time, my friend: stop wasting your life away and start living it consciously.

Essentialism

Are you familiar with the Pareto Principle?

Also known as the 80/20 rule, it's one of the most commonly cited principles in business and self-improvement literature.

This rule states that 80 percent of your results depend on just 20 percent of your work.

Here are a few common examples of how this rule applies:

- 80 percent of a store's profits come from just 20 percent of its customers

- 80 percent of a company's workload is completed by just 20 percent of its employees

- 80 percent of a software application's user base will utilize just 20 percent of its features

In other words, there are always a few key factors that determine the majority of the results.

While this rule can be applied to companies and businesses, it can also be applied to your personal life:

- 80 percent of your money is spent on just 20 percent of your interests

- 80 percent of your wasted time is spent on just 20 percent of your bad habits

- 80 percent of your thoughts are focused on just 20 percent of your life

The implications of this rule are that you can drastically improve your results by focusing on the key 20 percent of things that really matter.

You can save a lot of money by avoiding the 20 percent of things you spend the most on. You can free up a lot of time by avoiding the 20 percent of bad habits you waste the most time on. You can be a lot happier by refusing to engage in negative self-talk about the 20 percent of your life you tend to worry about the most.

Basically, less is more. By focusing on key areas, or key activities, you can quickly achieve a lot of big wins in your life.

And many studies have been done to back this up. One experiment was performed in 1996 on a group of college students in the *Journal of Education Psychology*. The students were shown a series of illustrations and text describing the process by which lightning occurs. Students who were shown just the illustrations and brief summaries had more success solving comprehension problems than students who were shown the illustrations and longer, more detailed explanations. [10]

When given less information, the students performed better. The additional information presumably cluttered the students' brains and prevented them from focusing on the key facts that were actually important. By reducing the amount of information they had to process, they were able to learn more and score higher marks.

Another study, this one published in the *Journal of Personality and Social Psychology* in 2000, depicts a similar trend. In this study, consumers were presented with the option to buy gourmet chocolates. Some were shown just 6 choices, while others were given 24 or 30 different choices. The consumers who were shown just 6 choices were more likely to purchase something, and they also reported being more satisfied with their decision afterward. [11]

Just like the students, these customers performed better and made better decisions when presented with less information. These studies demonstrate that you are more decisive – and more effective – when you have fewer options to process. You can focus better and achieve better results when there are fewer things to worry about.

A final study that I find particularly interesting on this subject was conducted by the *University of California* in 1997. This study investigated the link between innovation and company rules. After comparing the rules and regulations of many top companies, the study concluded that the presence of too many rules thwarted innovation and limited the expression of new and original ideas by employees. [12]

In other words, having a large number of rules that your employees have to comply with will ultimately prevent them from expressing their creativity and coming up with innovative ideas.

Again, the implications are clear: you simply cannot function at your highest level when you have to keep track of too many different things. If you can eliminate clutter, and focus on what really matters, you will always perform better.

Mindset #6: The less there is to worry about, the more I can focus on what really matters, and the better I can perform.

Our lives get more and more cluttered as we get older and older...

You buy more and more possessions that you have to keep track of. You meet more and more people that you have to keep in touch with. You acquire more and more responsibilities that you need to keep up with.

All of these things, people, and responsibilities distract you from doing the most important things in your life. Pointless purchases and hefty mortgages deplete your bank account. They prevent you from having the freedom to take vacations or start your own business. Work commitments and bad habits deplete your time. They prevent you from cultivating your most important relationships and enjoying your favorite hobbies.

All the while your life passes by. You try and consume too many different things, and then you end up sacrificing your most important dreams.

I got a painful reminder of this just last summer when I decided to move to Spain for a few months. I wanted a change of scenery, plus my parents and my brother live over there and I wanted to be closer to them for a bit.

However, my apartment lease was up in Boston and I hadn't planned what I was going to do with all of my stuff. After panicking for several weeks, I decided to do a massive purge instead of renewing my lease or putting everything into storage.

I thought it would be simple. I would sell some furniture, give some clothes away, and boom! That's all it would take...

Boy was I wrong! Some furniture, like my bedframe and dresser, sold quickly on Craigslist. However, some items, like my desk and sofa, did not. Some of my clothing items, like old underwear and cheesy t-shirts, were easy to ditch. However, some items, like expensive dress shirts or childhood sports jerseys, were almost impossible to part with.

This is not to mention all of the pointless BS I simply had to throw in the garbage. As I tossed old video cables and computer games into the dumpster, I felt guilty and wasteful.

But eventually I was done. I had given away about 75 percent of my clothing. I had sold or trashed all of my furniture. And I had thrown away just about everything else I owned, aside from my laptop and a few other essentials.

And you know what? I felt amazing. I literally felt happier than I had been in years!

By giving away all of these things, almost all of which I'd paid my hard earned money to get, I felt like I was finally free from years of consumerism and holding on to the past. I only owned clothes that I actually loved to wear, and possessions I actually needed to live. Everything else was gone. And it didn't hurt that I made some decent spending money in the process.

No longer did I need to spend time maintaining all of these things. No longer did I need to find space for storing them. I was finally free from their burden. I even decided to sell my car at the last minute, just one day before I hopped on the plane.

Since then, I've moved back to Boston, rented a new apartment, and furnished it. But this time around I avoided accumulating all of unnecessary BS I used to own. I even decided not to buy a new car. Between the subway, Uber, and my bike I can get anywhere I need to go. And I don't have to worry about parking, car insurance, getting gas, or any of that other BS.

When you combine that with the fact that I don't have a bunch of extra clothes to sort through every day, or a bunch of random video cables and old memorabilia I have to find space to store, it has made a huge difference in my ability to stay focused on the things that matter to me most.

Look, I'm not telling you to sell all of your possessions and move to Spain. I'm just stressing how important it is to free yourself of all the pointless "things" that you've accumulated over the years.

You have to escape the mindset that "more is better". Because, as these studies prove, less is better. The fewer things you need to keep track of, the more you can focus on what really matters, and the better you will perform.

Here are a few questions to get you thinking about how you can apply this mindset to your life:

What 20 percent of your possessions really matter?

Can you sell or give away the rest?

What 20 percent of your hobbies bring you the most joy? Can you dedicate more time to those?

What 20 percent of people do you enjoy seeing the most? Can you spend more time with them?

What 20 percent of the day are you most productive? Can you remove any distractions during that time?

Audit your life and decide on some key areas to focus more attention on.

Even if it means you need to discard some things or spend less time doing others, this process will immediately increase your happiness, productivity, and freedom.

Part II: Relationships

"The individual has always had to struggle to keep from being overwhelmed by the tribe. If you try it, you will be lonely often, and sometimes frightened. But no price is too high to pay for the privilege of owning yourself."

- Friedrich Nietzsche

Insecurity

Do you ever feel like you're the only one in the room who feels awkward or nervous?

Yes, well so do the rest of us.

Even today, years since my days of intense social anxiety, I still frequently feel "out of place" in certain social environments. Everybody does.

For example, just a few weeks ago I met up with my buddy at his friend's party. As I walked alone into a stranger's apartment, I realized that he and his girlfriend were the only two people I knew there. And I've only really met his girlfriend once or twice before.

Immediately I noticed a sense of anxiety. As he introduced me to a room full of people, I smiled and awkwardly waved at everyone.

"Fuck," I thought, "Why am I feeling so nervous right now?"

As thoughts of self-doubt started to play out inside my head, I caught myself. I stopped and focused on breathing deep breaths for a moment so I could get out of my head.

Before you know it, I was laughing, talking to new people, and having a good time. After hanging out for an hour or two at the apartment, we all headed out and hit some bars.

In the past, things would have been different. I would have engaged those negative thoughts, clung to my friend, avoided talking to new people, and most likely headed home when we left the apartment (rather than joining everyone else at the bar).

And you know what? Everyone else deals with these same issues.

One coaching client of mine would continually go to a weekend run club with the intention of meeting new people. After the run, everyone grabs coffee at a local café and talks to each other. My client would go for the run, go to the coffee shop, order a coffee, and then stand around for a few minutes before getting anxious and heading home (without taking to a single person).

Another client of mine would go out to bars in order to meet women. However, as soon as he got there he would be so nervous that he would anxiously alternate between ordering drinks at the bar and using the bathroom. He would get blacked out drunk without talking to a single person. He thought everyone was watching him, so he kept ordering drinks and using the bathroom in order to appear like he wasn't "weird" or "creepy".

Everybody is self-conscious on some level, and numerous studies have been done to confirm this truth. One study investigated suicide and depression rates among a group of male college graduates over a 27-year period. I'll also mention that these were graduates of Harvard University, perhaps the most prestigious school in the United States.

While you probably would not expect these successful men to become depressed or commit suicide, several hundred of them succumbed to both of these unfortunate outcomes. [13]

While this is an extreme example, and it's also quite sad, the point is that everyone is self-conscious. We are all prone to intense anxiety and depression. Everyone, no matter how successful or confident they appear, deals with insecurities and nervousness on a daily basis.

Another study investigated how a group of 67 college women reacted to seeing photos of thin female models on a screen. Those who saw the photos scored significantly higher on self-consciousness questionnaire when compared with a separate group of girls who were shown unrelated images. [14]

In other words, seeing thin female models made these women feel self-conscious and insecure.

While these studies don't definitively prove that

everyone is self-conscious – that's impossible to prove unless you figure out how to conduct a study on every living human – they do show definitive proof that many people experience anxiety, insecurity, and depression on a regular basis.

Mindset #7: Everybody is self-conscious.

It's true: everyone is self-conscious. Everyone walks around trying to portray a picture-perfect image to the world. But on the inside, they're freaking out. They're worrying about how you're looking at them. They're worrying about what you're thinking about them.

Let this knowledge free you! Realize that everyone is too busying worrying about themselves to be judging you.

The number one reason you get stuck in your head and over-analyze how you're acting in social environments is because you're worried about what other people think about you. You believe that everyone is judging you and looking down on you.

You must break free from this toxic mindset! And the fastest way to do so is to realize just how self-conscious everyone else is. Not only is this an effective mindset that will allow you to be far more confident in social situations, it's also 100% true.

Since birth, we're conditioned to worry about how we're perceived by other people. Our parents are often worried about how they look in public. Our school systems glorify being "cool" and popular. Every aspect of our culture, from television shows to internet advertisements, pressure us into living up to specific measures of success and attractiveness. And all of these factors combine to make us self-conscious.

So next time you find yourself in a crowded social environment, worrying about how stupid or how shy you look, stop and take a look around you.

Seriously, take a moment to stop worrying about yourself, and instead observe the room:

- *Catch yourself engaging in negative self-talk*

- *Breathe deeply and relax your shoulders*

- *Now look around and slowly analyze other people in the room*

Now that you're calmed down, see if you can spot a few other people who are being self-conscious.

And don't be fooled by your old mindset here. Just because nobody is collapsing on the floor in an all-out panic attack, that doesn't mean that they aren't extremely uncomfortable.

Notice people who are standing there and anxiously

looking around. Notice people who are nervously talking at 100 miles per hour. Notice people who are constantly going to the bathroom. Notice people who are neurotically checking their phones.

All of these people are likely worried how they look and what other people are thinking about them. Everyone is… even the smoking hot girl surrounded by a bunch of dudes… even the "alpha male" businessman in the expensive suit.

You must realize that everyone is self-conscious. You must realize that other people aren't always judging you. You must realize that you're not alone. And then you must let these realizations free you.

Compassion

Do you consider yourself to be a generous person?

There's a large body of evidence detailing how giving things to other people affects your mental and emotional psychology.

For example, a 2008 study published in the *Science* journal investigated how spending money on other people affects happiness. [15]

It had two major findings:

- People who spend a larger percentage of their income on others are measurably happier

- People who were randomly assigned to spend money on others experienced greater happiness than people who were randomly assigned to spend money on themselves

In other words, the study proved that spending money on other people makes you happy, regardless of whether or not it was even your choice to spend the money in the first place.

This is pretty powerful information. The first part of the study – that spending money on others generally leads to higher levels of happiness – is no big surprise. It just makes sense. People who regularly give money to others are more likely to be focused on the pain and suffering of other people. They're less likely to be caught up in their own issues and stuck in their own heads feeling sorry for themselves.

But the second part of the study is very interesting, not to mention a bit surprising. If you were forced to spend money on other people, not by your own choice, do you think it would make you feel happier?

I can't read your mind, but I'm guessing your answer is no. And that's nothing to be ashamed of, my answer is also no.

But this study proved the exact opposite! People who were randomly assigned to spend money on other people reported being happier than people who were randomly assigned to spend money on themselves.

Why do you think this is?

There's no way to know for sure, but in my mind, there are two distinct possibilities. First, maybe humans genuinely thrive off of the act of giving. Maybe our brains are simply wired to release dopamine when we give to others. Second, maybe these people received some compensation or benefit in reciprocation for the money they spent on other people. And maybe the happiness was a result of whatever they got in return.

However, the subjects in this study were interviewed soon after they were instructed to spend money on others. The likelihood of them receiving anything in return by this point is extremely small. Also, many of them donated the money to charities, and therefore did not receive anything more than a routine "thank you".

While this is not 100% definitive proof, it seems almost certain that we naturally feel happier after giving to others. It's a built-in response. We thrive off of giving.

However, very few of us act accordingly. Very few people genuinely care about the happiness and success of other people. Most people are only concerned with their own well-being. Most people are so worried about their own problems that they fail to lend a helping hand to other people. And when they do, they usually expect something in return.

Maybe you buy your girlfriend flowers, in hopes of getting her to forgive you for something. Maybe you help your friend move into his new apartment, in hopes that he will return the favor when you need help moving. Maybe you give someone a compliment, in hopes of them returning the favor and complimenting you.

None of these are true gifts. They will not make you happier. If you fail to receive whatever you were hoping for, then you're going to be pissed off. You weren't really giving a gift at all. You were just trying to get something out of them.

In the end, this is no better than NOT giving anything in the first place. In fact, it's actually worse. Not only do you fail to reap the happiness boost that comes along with genuine giving, but you also set yourself up for disappointment. If the favor is not returned, you're going to be let down.

Even worse, these types of "gifts" often create long-term resentment between you and the person you're dealing with. When they fail to reciprocate, you feel bitter towards them. And then you either get angry with them or begin to act in a passive-aggressive manner. And then the relationship deteriorates. All because you didn't receive compensation for your "favor".

Mindset #8: I genuinely want other people to be happy and successful.

This is not a simple mindset shift to make, I'll be honest.

We are all inherently selfish people. Yes, that includes you. And me.

And that's okay, it only makes sense. You live your own life. You need to look out for your own well-being. Your life and your happiness are your responsibility.

And that's exactly why it's so important to realize that giving to other people will boost your happiness. By giving to other people, and not expecting anything in return, you are actually looking out for your own good.

Not only that, but it also will boost the happiness of whoever you're helping. It's the definition of a win-win scenario. You're happier, they're happier, everybody wins.

So then all I have to do is make an effort to help other people?

Well, yes and no. Yes, you should make an effort to help other people when you see an opportunity. But honestly, the real key to making this mindset shift is catching yourself doing "favors" for other people in hopes of getting something in return.

Yes, you should absolutely think about what you can do to help others. You should think of what you can do to motivate your friends to improve their lives. You should think about what you can do to support your family members in living healthy lives. You should think about what you can contribute to society to make people's lives easier.

You should do more than think about these things, you should actually do them. It will create stronger relationships. It will help lift these people up so they can live bolder, stronger, richer lives. And if you can find a way to help lots of strangers solve their problems, it will also give you the ability to start your own business.

But more importantly, you need to catch yourself when you're doing something for someone else in hopes of getting something in return. You need to avoid this trap at all costs. Otherwise, it will cripple your confidence, your happiness, and your relationships.

If you only buy people gifts when you want them to forgive you or do something for you, then you will lose their trust. You will condition your girlfriend or wife to get mad at you, just so she can reap the benefits of getting a nice gift. You will condition your friends and family to do the same. It will ruin these relationships.

Do you really want to be the guy that has to buy a girl a drink, or some flowers, in order to get her attention? Do you really want to be the friend that has to throw an expensive party, or have access to an exclusive nightclub, in order to have company and feel wanted?

As author Robert Glover put it in his bestselling book *No More Mr. Nice Guy*: these are essentially "covert contracts". You're basically telling people. "Look, I'm doing this for you, but you have to do something for me in return." Except you're not actually telling them what you want from them.

You're saying, "Look, I'm too weak to be upfront with you, tell you how I really feel, and ask you for what I want. So I'm going to give you this, and I'm just going to hope that you get the message. I'm just going to hope that you read my mind and do what I want you to. And if not, I'm going to be pissed."

Can't you see how weak and pathetic that is?

Recognize the weakness in this mindset and stop doing it. Instead, actually help other people. Genuinely wish for their success and happiness. And then, when you need help, just ask for it.

Don't beat around the bush. Just be direct. Just be honest.

And then everyone wins. You actually help other people overcome challenges and obstacles in their own lives, rather than giving them "fake" gifts. And you actually ask for help or support when you need it. No strings attached.

Censorship

How often do you "hold your tongue" and decide not to say something?

Maybe you're afraid it will be too boring or mundane. Maybe you're afraid it will fail to impress the person you're talking you. Or maybe you're afraid it will offend them. Maybe you don't speak up because you don't want to create a confrontation.

This is extremely common. We all censor the words that come out of our mouths. However, is this really a smart thing to do?

Back when I was extremely insecure talking to women and expressing my sexuality, I would filter almost everything I said. I was deathly afraid that I was going to come off as too boring or too weird, and scare the girl off.

I remember one time, years ago, I was walking to the subway, and a cute girl was walking a few strides ahead of me. As I got to the subway station, she entered it as well. And once I navigated down the escalators and found the correct platform to wait at, she was there too. I wanted to talk to her so badly but I couldn't think of anything to say.

After 5 minutes of waiting, the train finally arrived. When the doors opened, I walked in and sat down in an empty seat. Seconds later, she sat down directly next to me.

"Fuck!" I thought, "Now I have to say something."

So I turned to her and said, "Hey there. I noticed we entered the subway together, waited together, and also ended up sitting together," while letting out a nervous laugh.

She turned to me, laughed, and said, "You're right, that is pretty funny."

Then I froze, as I always would. "Should I ask her how her day is going?" I thought. "No, that's so boring." I decided. "Maybe I should tell her I think she's cute?" I wondered. "No, it would be weird if I said that and she didn't like it. Then we'd be stuck here together anyway."

As I thought of different possible things to say to her, I shot them all down, one by one. Nothing was "good" enough.

So we sat there in silence. And eventually, about 15 minutes later, she got up, smiled, and said, "This is my stop. Have a nice day!"

I looked up and mumbled, "You too," before looking back down at the floor in defeat. I was ashamed. Yet again I failed to start a real conversation.

And it was 100% because I was censoring myself. I could have said any of the things I thought of and it would have gone better. Literally saying anything would have been better than sitting there and saying nothing.

But, again, I was afraid that I didn't have anything "good enough" to say.

Now let's contrast this with a similar situation I experienced more recently. This one happened just a few short months ago.

Again, I was walking to the subway station. This time, I was all alone. However, once I found my way to the correct platform, I spotted a cute girl waiting there alone. I found a seat that was within talking distance and sat down.

Sitting there, I decided I would talk to her. Best case I get a date, worst case I kill some time. But what to say?

"Hmmm," I thought, "I haven't taken this subway line before, maybe I'll ask her how long my trip will take."

Without giving it a second thought, I turned to her and asked, "Hey, do you know how long it takes to get to the Riverside station from here? I've never taken this line before."

She turned and said, "I honestly don't know. I live a

few stops away so I've never been that far before."

"Damn," I thought, "She's not giving me much to work with."

So I paused for a second and then followed up, "Oh I gotcha. Well, how long does it take to get to your stop? Are the stops very far apart?"

She laughed, presumably at my weak attempt to keep the conversation going, and said, "No it's pretty quick. Only about 5 minutes or so. Why are you going all the way to Riverside?"

I smiled. Despite my lame question, she opened up and asked me a question.

"My parents recently moved near there and I'm heading over to see them for the weekend," I replied. "Are you heading home from work or what?"

Again, I asked a rather mundane question, but it was the first thing that popped into my head.

The conversation continued like this for a few minutes, before we got comfortable enough to joke around and tease each other. She ended up having a boyfriend, but it was still nice to meet someone new and have some company for the first part of my trip.

The only difference between this story and the first story is that I didn't censor myself this time around. I didn't filter my thoughts. I just said whatever came into my head, no matter how boring it seemed.

Mindset #9: I am happier, more confident, and more attractive when I express myself unapologetically.

Look, I know neither of these stories is particularly noteworthy. The point is that I failed to start a conversation the first time around, all because I censored myself.

This is a simple mindset shift that can have a huge impact on your social confidence.

If you filter your thoughts and prevent yourself from speaking your mind, this is most likely a habit you've developed over time. You've probably convinced yourself that you're "bad" at conversation. Or that you're a boring person. Or that you aren't witty enough to speak boldly to strangers.

It's all BS. None of this is true. You've simply become comfortable filtering your thoughts and censoring the words that come out of your mouth.

We are all inherently proficient at talking to others. That includes you. You have the ability to have consistently amazing conversations with anyone. And I'm sure that deep down you know this. I'm sure that you've experienced many instances when you were able to talk to strangers with complete confidence. I'm sure that you've experienced times when you were able to "turn off" your thoughts and just let the words flow through you.

Well here's the thing: you have the ability to do this every single day, regardless of who you're speaking to. You simply have to stop filtering your thoughts.

It's going to be a little intimidating to do this at first. You've probably done such a good job at convincing yourself that almost everything is too boring – or too weird – to say. But now you must de-condition this toxic mindset.

What's the fastest way to do this? Simple:

- Catch yourself the next time that you get "locked up" censoring yourself in conversation

- Say the next thing that pops into your head

- Now stop talking and let the other person respond

- Repeat this process

At first, this is going to feel awkward. You're not going to want to speak your mind. You're going to want to find the "perfect" thing to say.

This is normal. But you have to push through and do it anyway.

At first, you're probably going to say some boring things. That is also normal. If you keep going, I promise that you will quickly break through this boring small talk. You will quickly start to have genuinely fun, free-flowing conversations. You just need to learn to trust yourself.

In the next chapter, we'll discuss another key mindset for having consistently amazing conversations. If you combine these two mindsets, you will become an unstoppable conversationalist. I promise.

Empathy

What do you focus on when you're talking to someone else?

If you're like most people, you're usually focused on relating what the other person is talking about back to yourself. When they finish talking, you tell them about a similar experience you had or something like that.

Or maybe you're just plain worried about what you're going to say next, and you're always trying to think of the "right" thing to say.

Both of these mindsets are very common. In fact, I would say that they're the norm. It's simply how most people operate inside of a conversation. We hear the other person out, talk a little about ourselves, and then it's their turn again. But there's a better way...

You see, research has recently confirmed that you experience pleasure when you talk about yourself. Talking about yourself – or self-disclosure – is strongly associated with increased activation in certain parts of the brain, including the nucleus accumbens and ventral tegmental area. [16]

These areas combine to form the mesolimbic-dopamine system, also known as the "reward pathway". When you talk about yourself, you activate these areas of the brain, and then you feel pleasure as a result.

While that's pretty damn amazing, it makes complete sense. Think about it: what do you do when something drastic happens to you in life?

It doesn't matter if it's something good, like getting a promotion or getting engaged, or something bad, like a getting dumped or a getting diagnosed with a chronic disease. Regardless, you want to tell other people about it. You want them to know about your success. Or your pain.

Even on a day-to-day basis, you like to tell other people about your day. What happened at work today? What did you eat for lunch? What crazy video did you see on Facebook?

Face it: you love telling people about your life. And here's the thing: everybody else is the same. We all love talking about ourselves.

Why is this so significant? Good question.

This is so significant because it should change how you approach conversation. Rather than jumping back and forth between talking about yourself and talking about the other person, you can focus fully on them. After all, that's what they want to do, even if they don't know it.

Rather than talking a little bit about your day, and then letting them talk a little bit about their day, you can skip past the BS and focus fully on them. Not only will this make them feel good about themselves, but it will allow the conversation to reach a deeper level.

Rather than skimming the surface about what you both want to talk about, you can dive deep into their day, their passions, and their interests. This will make them happy. This will allow you to learn more about them. And here's the amazing part: this will actually make them like you more.

They will begin to associate these feelings of pleasure with talking to you. They will begin to see you as someone who actually cares about them. And this will separate you from everyone else who just tries to talk about themselves.

Mindset #10: I can learn something from everyone I talk to.

This is the key mindset to adopt here.

You don't just want to talk about the other person because I told you so. You want to actually take an interest in their life, and see what you can learn from them. Everyone has unique experiences and unique interests. By focusing the conversation on them you can learn a lot.

A few weeks ago, I was hanging out with my girlfriend (now my ex) and her friends. One of them was a guy who works at a brewery making beers. I love beer, but I know very little about it.

So I started to learn from him. I asked what his favorite type of beer was. I asked what his favorite brand of beer was. I asked why. I asked how he got into brewing beer.

Side note: always ask people about how they got into their occupation. It will tell you a lot about them, and everyone loves to tell this story.

I quickly learned the difference between different types of beers. I learned about what beers I should try, based on my current preferences. And I learned this guy's life story.

The amazing thing is that I didn't have to think at all. I simply listened to him and encouraged him to keep talking about himself. I could see his eyes light up as he explained how the United States only taxes beer companies on the finished product, while European countries tend to tax based on the ingredients that go into the beer. "That's why US beers tend to have higher alcohol content," he told me. He was thoroughly enjoying our talk.

And you know what? He eventually reciprocated. He eventually began to ask me about my life, my hobbies, and my business.

People always do. After you show a genuine interest in their life, they will get tired talking about themselves, and get curious about you. They will start to ask you question-after-question about your life, your interests, and your passions.

And then you get to talk about yourself. You get to activate those same pleasure centers in your brain. You get to feel good about yourself.

Before you know it, you'll be having the deepest conversations of your life... with everyone you talk to. You'll be forming genuinely deep, long lasting connections with everyone you meet.

Here's the simple recipe for using this technique to dominate any conversation:

- Ask the other person a question about their life

- Listen to their answer, don't worry about what you're going to say next

- When they finish, encourage them to keep talking about themselves

That's literally all it takes.

If you do this, you will quickly get good at asking the right types of questions. You will quickly learn how to open people up. And they will love you for it.

And you know what? You're going to love them, too.

Boundary

Do you have strong boundaries? Or do you let people walk all over you?

Be honest with yourself here. This can be a painful thing to admit.

No one wants to be that guy who gets dragged around by his girlfriend, his wife, or his boss. No one wants to be seen as the guy who nobody really respects...

Yet most of us still fail to set strong boundaries. Most of us fail to have well-defined limits that we demand other people to respect, regardless of the situation.

What exactly are boundaries? I'll give you a few examples to show you what I'm talking about.

Let's say that your girlfriend cheats on you. How do you react? You probably get pissed off and break up with her. She slept with another guy, and you can no longer trust her. She violated your boundary, so you must walk away.

But let's say you don't. Let's say you just get pissed at her, but you're too weak or too afraid to break up with her. You threaten to do it, but ultimately you pussy out and stay with her. You tell yourself that you love her and that you will "figure things out".

You failed to set a strong boundary. You know that she crossed the line and that you should break up with her, but you can't bring yourself to do it.

What are the consequences here?

Well, there are two main consequences. First of all, your girlfriend is going to lose respect for you. She knows that she crossed the line and that you failed to follow through on your threats to break up with her. Even if she truly loves you, she can no longer trust you to live up to your word and honor your boundaries.

Second, you are going to lose respect for yourself. You know that she crossed the line and that cheating is something that's completely unacceptable to you in a relationship. But you couldn't bring yourself to honor this boundary. You couldn't bring yourself to walk away. The cost of losing her ultimately seemed greater to you than the need to respect yourself. And that shit hurts... worse than a breakup.

Not only is she more likely to cross your boundaries again in the future, because she knows you're too weak to walk away, but you're also more likely to feel resentment towards her going forward. Not to mention, you're also more likely to feel resentment towards yourself.

I used the example of cheating because that's

something that's clearly over the line for most people. It's black and white. Cheating is wrong. It's an irreparable breach of trust.

But the real problem lies in the gray area. The real problem lies when you fail to identify your personal boundaries.

For example, if your boss asks you to stay 30 minutes late one day, is that okay? For most people, it's an inconvenience, but not a reason to quit.

But what if he asks you to come into work every Saturday? For most people, this would be an issue. Maybe you decide that it's okay, assuming that your boss compensates you for the extra time. But maybe you decide that working on the weekends simply isn't acceptable. You simply value your day off more than he's willing to compensate you.

Regardless of what you decide, you must follow through and honor your boundary. You must demand compensation. Or you must say no. You must say no and be prepared to quit, or at least to go find another job, if he does not respect this boundary.

If not, your boss will lose respect for you. He will know that you're too weak to say no to him. He will continue to take advantage of you.

And you will constantly be angry at him, and show obvious signs of resentment.

Not to mention, you will feel like shit about yourself. You will know that he's taking advantage of you, but that you're too weak to do anything about it.

Mindset #11: Certain things should not be tolerated.

This is a tough mindset to adopt, I'm not going to lie.

Letting go is the most difficult thing you can do. It doesn't matter if this means walking away from your girlfriend, your wife, your job, or your friend. The fear of losing things that we already have is one of the most paralyzing fears there is.

But in order to set strong boundaries you have to be willing to let go. You have to be willing to say, "Look, you crossed the line. I will not tolerate this behavior or this request." And then you must walk away.

Otherwise, you will fail to create the life you truly want. If your girlfriend, your wife, your boss, or your friend is comfortable walking all over you, you will never truly be happy with yourself.

The only way to find a girlfriend, a boss, or a friend who truly respects you and adds value to your life is to be prepared to walk away when they do something that you've decided is unacceptable.

Let me make one thing clear: I'm not saying to hold everyone to unreasonably high standards. I'm not saying to break up with your girlfriend or divorce your wife if she shows up late to dinner. I'm not saying to stop hanging out with your life-long friend if he insults you or makes fun of you. I'm not saying to quit your job if your boss asks you to put in a little extra time.

No, you need to be flexible. There's never going to be a moment when everything is 100% perfect in your life. You simply need to decide what's acceptable to you and what's not. What behaviors or actions are crossing your personal boundaries? What behaviors or actions cannot be tolerated?

If you fail to do this, and you fail to honor these boundaries, you will set the precedent that you're too weak to walk away. You will betray the trust of other people because they're silently cheering for you to stand up for yourself, whether they know it or not.

And you will also betray your own self-respect. You will fail to build trust in yourself to make the hard decisions when needed.

You must avoid this trap at all costs. Recognize when other people cross the line. Remind yourself of the long-term consequences of letting it go. Then confront them and speak your mind.

Don't antagonize them, but let them know exactly how you feel. Then act accordingly, even if this means walking away.

Validation

Whose love and approval do you value the most?

Maybe it's your father's. Maybe it's your boss's. Maybe it's your best friend's.

But, if you're like most guys, then you probably seek approval from two main sources: your friends and attractive women.

You probably want to look good in front of your friends. You want to be a cool guy and get their respect. And you probably want to feel desired by women, too. You want to feel wanted.

Most guys spend their entire lives seeking approval from these two categories of people. You try and get jobs that pay you a lot of money so you can feel important. You spend that money on cool clothes and expensive cars so that other people recognize your importance.

You want to be respected by other men. You want to be desired by attractive women.

You brag to your friends about all the women you've slept with. And you brag to women about all the cool experiences you've had.

You want to be respected by other men. You want to be desired by attractive women.

You want to feel important. And these are two of the main ways that you try and get that feeling. When you get the approval that you're looking for, it makes you feel important. It makes you feel wanted.

When your friends listen to your stories and give you compliments, you feel respected. When women laugh at your jokes and sleep with you, you feel desired. And you like it.

You like it so much that you repeatedly try to feel these same emotions, over and over again. You repeatedly try and impress your friends. You repeatedly try and impress women. For most guys, it becomes the driving force in their lives. It becomes the reason they do everything that they do.

Why did you buy that fancy new car? Why did you post that photo on Instagram? Why did you tell your friend that story?

Be honest: were you trying to impress someone?

I'm guessing that the answer is yes. Maybe you had other motivations too, but that was almost definitely one of them.

Let me make one thing clear: I don't think seeking approval is inherently bad. It's human nature to want to be desired and respected by other people.

Growing up, all the way from pre-school to college graduation, you were conditioned to seek validation. After all, that's what separates the "cool" kids from the losers.

But it does help to be aware of it. Otherwise, you will be devastated and depressed whenever you fail to get the recognition you seek. You will feel like a worthless failure when a girl turns you down. Or when a guy makes fun of you.

You will feel rejected. You will feel sad. And you will begin to pity yourself.

But none of this is productive. None of this is healthy. None of this makes sense.

And even when you do get the approval you seek, you're still left wanting more. After you successfully get a girl to go on a date with you, are you completely satisfied? No, now you want to make sure you get a second date. Otherwise, you won't be happy. And even if you get the second date, are you completely satisfied? No, now you want to take her home and sleep with her. And even then, you won't be completely satisfied. Next, you will want to make her your girlfriend or ditch her and find another girl to sleep with.

No matter how much approval you get, you'll always want more. It's like a drug. As soon as the high wears off, you want another hit. You might think it will make you happy, but it never does.

Mindset #12: Living up to my own values is more important than getting approval from other people.

Clearly seeking validation from other people, be it guys or girls, is not an effective way to live your life. It can only lead to disappointment and anxiety.

So how do you overcome this toxic mindset?

Well, first you have to accept the fact that you enjoy getting approval. You have to accept that you've spent most of your life chasing it. And this can be a hard pill to swallow. We simply don't like to acknowledge that we've been doing something so wrong for so long.

And, after we recognize this truth, we need to learn how to get validation from within. We need to learn how to replace this need for external approval with our own inner sense of approval.

This is also not an easy task. But there is an effective way to accomplish this. It simply requires making one crucial mindset shift. It simply requires that we strive to live up to our own expectations and values, rather than the expectations and values of everyone else.

Think about it this way: right now you're trying to impress other people. You think that by impressing other people, and getting their subsequent approval, it will make you happy. And it does make you happy. But the happiness doesn't last. There's always someone else's approval you need to get.

Think about it like this...

Imagine that you were a car. You need gas to keep going. But you can only get gas at gas stations. In this analogy, you are the car and gas stations are other people. Now, paying for gas represents getting their approval. Once you fill up, you're good for a bit longer. But eventually, you will need more gas in order to feel happy and loved.

But what if you put a solar panel on your car? Now the car is self-powered. It can keep going on and on without needing gas. This is essentially what happens when you learn to self-validate. You no longer need approval from other people to feel good about yourself. You are now able to supply yourself with all of the love and happiness you'll ever need.

Now, that's great analogy and all, but how do I actually accomplish this?

Good question.

Before I give you the exact breakdown of what you need to do, let's take a look at a study published in the *Journal of Research in Personality* back in 2003. This study took a group of 180 college students (half men, half women) and had them fill out a brief questionnaire.

Inside the questionnaire, they rated the importance of five distinct characteristics: intelligence, physical attractiveness, material possessions, humor, and morality. Afterward, they rated themselves on how well they compared to their peers in each category.

Now here's the important part. After that, each student completed a self-esteem evaluation.

When the researchers analyzed the results, they found that subjects who rated themselves well – in categories they felt were important – had higher self-esteem on average. [17]

The findings of this study are extremely profound. It proves that living up to your own values leads to higher confidence and self-esteem.

You see, the mistake most people make is trying to live up to other people's values. You try and impress other people to feel good about yourself. But that's not effective because that's not how self-esteem really works.

Sure, living up to someone else's values and getting their approval will give you a temporary boost in confidence and happiness. But it does not lead to increased confidence or happiness in the long run. No, in order to actually improve your self-esteem you need to live up to your own values.

So how do you do this? It's actually pretty straightforward, you just need to do a quick self-assessment:

- List out your top 10-20 values

- Decide which 5 are most important to you

- Rate yourself (from 1-10) in each category, be brutally honest

- For the categories where you rate poorly, think of how you can improve your rating

For example, if you value courage and bravery, but you think you're kind of a wimp, then you need to figure out how you can become more courageous. Maybe this means picking up a martial art. Maybe this means asking a girl out. Maybe this means quitting your job.

I can't tell you what your values are. And I can't tell you exactly what you need to do to live up to them.

But I can tell you that I've done this exercise with hundreds of friends, family members, and coaching clients. And I can tell you that it works. It will make you feel way better about yourself. It will help you stop chasing validation and approval.

If you're struggling to think of values, here are a few to help get your juices flowing: courage, honesty, compassion, intelligence, competence, humor, strength, growth, creativity, independence, leadership, decisiveness, style, authenticity, competitiveness, comradery, passion, energy, health, fitness, adventure, love, companionship, friendliness.

Part III: Achievement

"You can't connect the dots looking forward; you can only connect them looking backwards. So you have to trust that the dots will somehow connect in your future. You have to trust in something - your gut, destiny, life, karma, whatever."

- Steve Jobs

Passion

Do you pursue your passions in life? Or do you just follow the path of least resistance?

Steve Jobs, the founder of Apple, is widely considered the most innovative entrepreneur of his generation.

Many people even use the word "genius" to describe his ability to consistently create groundbreaking products such as the iPod, the iPad, and the iPhone. These products literally revolutionized how we listen to music and how we communicate with each another.

Apple products have quickly changed how most of us live our lives. And this is why Apple has grown into the dominant brand that it is today.

Now, despite all of these historic accomplishments, one of Jobs' most memorable moments was an unforgettable commencement speech he delivered to the graduating class of Stanford University in Palo Alto, California on June 12, 2005.

In this speech he urged the attending student body – and millions upon millions of people who would later view the speech on YouTube – to find something they love in life, and then pursue it with reckless abandon.

He began the speech by telling an interesting story...

Back in 1972 – while Jobs was attending Reed College in Portland, Oregon – he decided to drop out. He simply wanted to take classes that actually interested him, rather than being forced to attend a bunch of boring, required ones.

One afternoon, after making this decision, he stopped by a calligraphy class. While sitting in on the class he learned a bit about how to draw characters using different, distinct styles.

Now this seemed pretty insignificant at the time. He was simply curious about the class. But ten years later, when Jobs was preparing to release the first ever Macintosh computer, something interesting happened.

In the final stages of preparation, Jobs happened to remember his experience in that class. And it caused him to make an unprecedented decision: to include different styles of writing – different fonts – as an experimental feature for this new machine.

And this is how computer fonts – an innovation that we all still use today – came to be. Pretty crazy, right?

Well, here's the point of this whole story: if Jobs

didn't decide to sit in on that random calligraphy class back in 1972, he may have never had the unique insight he needed to invent computer fonts.

There's no way he could've planned for this. He didn't "connect the dots" looking forward and purposefully attend that calligraphy class so that he could later use the experience as inspiration to invent computer fonts. No, that would be impossible.

But he *was* able to "connect the dots" looking backward. He was able to remember a chance experience he had, no matter how irrelevant or unrelated it seemed at the time, and use it to his advantage.

This was the entire point of his speech. You cannot plan which "dots" in your life are going to be important down the road. You cannot plan exactly what you need to do in order to have the most success later on in life.

Instead, you should focus on pursuing things that you enjoy. You should focus on accumulating lots and lots of "dots" that are interesting and appealing to you. Then, later down the road, you give yourself the best chance to "connect the dots" and create something amazing.

Mindset #13: Pursuing my interests will make me happier now, and it can also lead to game-changing opportunities in the future.

Look, this doesn't mean you should drop out of college and start attending calligraphy classes... not unless you really want to.

But it does mean that you should pursue goals that you actually care about, rather than ones that you think "make the most sense" or ones that other people expect you to. By avoiding this pitfall, one that almost everyone falls into, you give yourself the best chance to find your passions and create a life that you're truly proud of.

Now let me give you an example from my life, just in case Steve Jobs' story doesn't seem so relatable for you.

I've been following this exact mindset, albeit unintentionally, for most of my life.

You see, playing video games and building computers were two of my main hobbies during my adolescence. While other high school kids were going out and getting drunk, I was at home installing water-cooling systems in my computers or dominating online multiplayer games in the original *Call of Duty*.

Sure, I was avoiding some deeper social issues, but I also genuinely loved computers. And this love drove me to study computer science at Boston University. And this led me to apply to tech-related jobs during my senior year. Before you knew it, I was working as a software engineer for a small tech company in Sudbury, Massachusetts.

I was embracing my interest for computers and collecting "dots" as I went.

While I was in school, I also began to embrace fitness and bodybuilding. It was essentially a replacement for the physical activity I got from playing football and basketball in high school. As I watched my body grow and adapt to the stressors of lifting weights, I became addicted.

I started studying exercise science and nutrition. I began counting my calories and tracking the exercises, weights, and repetitions I performed in the gym with complete precision. I set detailed goals to build more muscle and lift more weight.

Again, I was embracing my interest for fitness and collecting even more "dots".

After a full year of working behind a computer in a small cubicle, I decided I wanted a change. Every afternoon I felt sluggish and tired. The only part of my day I looked forward to was going to the gym on the way home. I took this as a sign to study up and get a personal trainer certification.

Against the advice of my friends and family members, who urged me to continue my career in software, I decided to quit my job and become a personal trainer. Yet again I was embracing my urge to follow my interests. Yet again I was collecting more "dots".

Now here's the part where all these dots start to connect.

Every night, after coaching clients in the gym all day, I found myself missing the "intellectually challenging" aspect of being an engineer. I was also reading lots of self-help books. And many of these books preached entrepreneurial ideals, urging me to try and start a "side hustle" – a small business I could run from home.

So one day I decided to create a website. I decided it was time to try and build something of my own. But what would it be?

After some thought, it was clear. I would create an online resource to help guys get in shape and build confidence in themselves. I used my tech background to teach myself some web design skills and build the website. I used my experience coaching clients in the gym to help me communicate clearly and effectively. And I used my passions for fitness and self-development as the main content for the site.

Now, this would not turn into a profitable business until several years later. But it's now my full-time job... and it all came together because of the many different "dots" I collected by pursuing my interests.

I'm able to work for myself, doing something I love, all because I pursued my constantly-changing interests over the past 5 or 10 years.

Look, I'm not trying to brag here. I didn't even do this on purpose. I was simply being impulsive and doing what felt right. But, as you can see, following this pattern consistently, year after year, is what allowed me to get to where I am today.

Now I must urge you to do the same. You must stop setting goals to get a specific promotion, or go on a certain vacation, just because that's what other people are trying to do. You must stop following in the footsteps of your friends and family members, just because that's what is expected of you. You must stop letting other people dictate what you choose to pursue in life.

Instead, you must listen to your gut. If you want to learn a new skill, then go for it. If you want to change careers, then do it. If you want to stop wasting your time doing something you don't really enjoy, then give it up already!

The only way to find your "passions" is to embrace your interests. Interests become passions when you embrace them and get good at them. So stop pussy-footing around and go all out!

If you live life unconsciously – and avoid collecting "dots" – then you're doomed to live a boring life. Seriously, if you keep doing what you're doing, then nothing is going to change.

As they say: doing the same thing over and over, but expecting different results, is the definition of insanity. So start doing shit that you genuinely love to do. Not only will it lead to short term happiness, but it will also lead to game-changing opportunities down the road.

Future

How far ahead do you plan? 1 month? 1 year? 5 years? 10 years?

A lot of people place a high degree of importance on planning ahead.

In fact, you've probably been asked the question: "What's your 5-year plan?" or "Where do you see yourself in 5 years?" multiple times in your life.

Maybe it was in a job interview. Maybe your father asked you. Maybe you heard it on a podcast or read it in a book. Either way, I'm sure that it made you stop and think for a minute.

Did you have a good answer?

If you're like most people then probably not. You probably reached into your mind, looked around, and came up with nothing.

"Uh, I guess I want to be better than I am today."

Even if you didn't say that, it's probably what was going through your head. After all, most of us simply aren't thinking that far ahead. So when you get asked that question, it can be kind of stressful.

"Shit, I should probably figure that out," you might be thinking.

At least that's what I was thinking when I started to hear that question during my final years of college. Just getting asked that question led me to falsely believe that everyone else had a detailed 5-year plan. It made me feel like a failure, at least on some level.

It was like everyone else knew exactly where they were headed, and I was about to get left behind.

But here's the thing: 5-year plans are pure BS. They assume that your life is going to continue on the exact same trajectory that you're on now – and let's be honest – that *never* happens.

Your interests will change. The economic conditions of the country will change. The geopolitical makeup of the entire world will change. The company you're working at right now will change. Your friends will change. Your romantic situation will change. Your family members will die.

Everything is going to fucking change! So how is a static, pre-determined 5-year plan going to help you? All it's going to do is give you a false sense of security. A false sense of control.

Look, I'm not saying that planning ahead is completely worthless. You should absolutely invest in a retirement account so your money grows over time. You should absolutely take amazing care of your body so you feel better, look better, and live longer. You should absolutely cultivate strong relationships that will continue to support you over time.

I'm not saying to be a short-sighted idiot, quit your job, travel the world, and do as many drugs as possible without any regard for your future. Sure, you might enjoy it for a bit. But soon enough your bank account is going to run out, your health is going to catch up with you, and you're going to be forced to face the music.

But I am saying that you shouldn't waste your time and energy creating detailed 5-year or 10-year plans to outline your desired future. Yes, I know that plenty of people will disagree with this statement, but keep reading. I will offer a superior alternative shortly.

Mindset #14: My next mission is the most important one.

The superior mindset is to focus fully on completing your next mission in life.

Throw your BS 5-year plan out the window, and gear up to take down your next mission with a fierce determination that will ensure it gets done efficiently and effectively.

I'll explain exactly how to implement this process at the end of the chapter, but for now just know that by "mission" I mean a short-term goal. By focusing on setting short-term goals that you can complete in 6 months or less, you will supercharge your productivity, your motivation, and your personal growth.

You will no longer risk the analysis-paralysis that comes along with planning too far ahead. The number of moving parts you need to account for is far less, and therefore you can focus fully on the crucial factors that make a difference right now.

This will boost your productivity big time because the risk for information overload is significantly diminished. Rather than worrying about how everything you're doing now is going to affect where you are in 5-years, you can fully immerse yourself in your work. The amount of daily stress that you sidestep in the process will have huge benefits on your work capacity and your work quality over time.

In other words, you're going to be able to get way more shit done and achieve way more of your goals.

Not only will this approach supercharge your productivity, but it will also drastically enhance your motivation. You see, when you plan too far ahead and set long-term goals, you're also delaying the payoff you'll receive when you finally accomplish the goal. And this decreases motivation.

Rather than being excited to get to work on your mission every single day, you will often lose sight of the end game. This kills motivation *and* productivity. Not only that, but it significantly increases the likelihood that you'll decide to completely give up and quit before reaching the finish line.

Finally, and most importantly, focusing fully on your next mission will supercharge your self-development. You see, when you set short-term goals, they're always going to be a reflection of your current interests and passions.

And, as we explored in the previous chapter, pursuing your current passions with reckless abandon is a huge predictor of your future success. Rather than ignoring your current passions and focusing on lofty, long-term goals, you should set short-term goals that allow you to embrace them and to collect more "dots" in the process.

As you complete mission after mission, you will gain experience and knowledge in a wide variety of domains that actually interest you. This puts you in the best possible position to "connect the dots" in the future and create a career for yourself that merges together several of your different passions.

This mindset is basically an extension of the previous one. This mindset allows you to actually implement the previous mindset and start pursuing your passions today.

Get started now by identifying a mission you can complete over the next few months.

This could mean that you decide to try a new hobby in your free time. This could mean that you decide to pursue a specific promotion at work. This could mean that you try and start a side-hustle or self-publish your own book on Amazon.

The main thing is that it's important to you and that you can complete it in 6 months or less.

March on, soldier, you now have your mission.

Focus

Do you struggle to follow through and achieve your goals?

Procrastination, lack of focus, bad luck, unforeseen inconvenience, sickness, injury, fatigue, travel, work, friends, family... the list goes on.

There are an infinite number of reasons you can fail to get something done. There are an infinite number of excuses you can make for failing to achieve a particular goal.

But there's only one real reason that you successfully accomplish something in life: you do the work. One-by-one, you take the steps necessary to get you from start to finish. The same way you need to physically put one foot in front of the other in order to complete a race, you need to physically do all of the action steps in order to complete anything in life.

It's so simple, yet so many of us fail to achieve the goals we set for ourselves. This number gets thrown around a lot, but it's true: only 8% of people successfully follow through on their New Year's resolutions...

That means that 92% of people who set New Year's

resolutions fail. [18]

92% of people who set a goal to lose weight, quit smoking, save money, learn something new, or start dating again fail to take the steps necessary to achieve their goal.

Those are 5 of the 10 most common New Year's resolutions, by the way. And all of these things are relatively simple to accomplish. It's not like these people are trying to start a business or cure cancer. They are trying to achieve relatively mundane things. They know exactly what they need to do, yet they still fail to do it.

Why is that?

Well, the number one excuse people give is that they "don't have enough time." But this is pure BS.

Not having enough time is not a reason to stuff a Snickers bar into your mouth. Not having enough time is not a reason to binge watch 8 hours of Netflix instead of going to the gym for 45 minutes. Not having enough time is not a reason to blow $200 on drinks every Friday night. Not having enough time is not a reason to smoke a pack of cigarettes every day.

No, the real reason we fail is because we don't really care about achieving the goal in the first place, or because we get overwhelmed and quit.

If you don't care about achieving a particular goal,

then you're doing it for the wrong reasons and you probably should quit. But if you actually care about achieving your goal – and you still quit – then you likely got overwhelmed.

Having to give up your favorite foods every single day for the next few 3 months can seem impossible. Having to go to the gym every other day for the rest of your life can seem intimidating. Having to give up cigarettes forever can seem unimaginable...

Having to take *all* of the steps necessary for achieving your goal can seem hopeless.

Setting short-term goals, like we explored in the previous chapter, will help a lot. But even then, the thought of having to follow through on your intentions every single day for several months can seem almost inconceivable.

When you start to think about everything you're going to need to do to get something done, you can quickly get overwhelmed. You can quickly build it up in your head to be a bigger sacrifice than it really is...

And this makes it *very* easy to throw in the towel and quit. This makes it very easy to find an excuse to not do the work you need to do. This makes it very easy to become complacent in life, drink another soda, watch another episode, and then go to sleep.

Mindset #15: All that matters is taking the next step, no matter how small it is.

The mindset you should adopt is to only worry about the very next physical step you need to take, no matter how tiny or how insignificant it seems.

This mindset will free you from the endless thoughts of how "hard" your life is going to be if you continue down the path of working towards a particular goal. This mindset will prevent you from becoming overwhelmed and deciding to quit.

I learned this mindset when I read *Getting Things Done* by David Allen. This bestselling book is widely considered the Bible of productivity. And the most important thing it preaches is to break down your goals into a series of "next action" steps.

This is so important because it allows you to skip past the procrastination that comes along with having to re-analyze your entire goal over and over again. Having to re-process everything you need to do each time that you get to work is a sure-fire recipe for failure. It leads to constant stress and anxiety.

But when you simply focus on the next physical action you need to take, you side-step this problem.

Rather than having to find new job opportunities, update your resume, write a bunch of cover letters, send a bunch of emails, do a bunch of interviews, and then maybe get a job offer, you only have to think about one small step: brainstorming one specific job title that might appeal to you, for example.

Rather than having to write an entire book, edit it, hire a graphic designer to illustrate the cover, and develop an intricate launch plan, you only have to think about one small step: outlining the first chapter, for example.

In fact, this methodology is the only way I've been able to self-publish over 8 books to date. I simply wake up each morning and get to work on the next step, trusting that everything will come together in the end...

Well, that's not completely true. Sometimes I get worked up. Sometimes I start to think about everything I need to do right in order to make sure this book is a success. And then I get stressed out. I even consider quitting. But eventually, I remind myself of this crucial mindset. "Forget about all that, David, just focus on the next step," I tell myself.

And then I get to work, get shit done, and eventually complete the book. And it usually hits the bestsellers list... all because I was able to set aside my doubts and focus on taking one small step at a time.

I even apply this mindset to help myself overcome

bad habits, or build good ones. For example, whenever I get the urge to text my ex-girlfriend, I simply tell myself, "Not this time, David. Just text her next week."

Or when I was building the habit of taking a cold shower every morning, I would tell myself, "Alright, just take this one cold shower today, tomorrow I can take the day off."

By breaking down these habits into small, singular actions I've been able to integrate them into my daily routine indefinitely. Rather than worrying about not being able to talk to my ex-girlfriend ever again, I just decide that I won't do it today. Rather than worrying about having to endure the pain of a cold shower every single morning for the rest of my life, I just decide that I'll do it just one more time.

Now it's your turn. You need to apply this same mindset to your life. Whenever you catch yourself getting overwhelmed by a large project, remind yourself that all you have to do right now is take one more small step.

For example, if you want to lose weight, your first 3 steps might be to download a calorie counting app, calculate your target daily calories, and then plug in everything you've eaten so far today into the app.

Or if you want to open a retirement account to invest in, your first 3 steps might be to see what options your employer offers, enter one of them into Google, and then read an article about how it works.

Remember, the smaller the better. After you've completed a few days of taking small steps you will begin to build some momentum, and that will drive you forward towards inevitable success.

Motivation

What motivates you? Why do you want the things you want? Why do you do the things you do?

Back when I was working as a personal trainer full-time, I had an organized system to identify the needs of my new clients.

Before they even purchased training with me, I would take them through a series of assessments so that I could understand their goals, determine their level of fitness, and see if working with me was a good fit.

The very first thing I did was to ask them, "What are your fitness goals? What motivated you to schedule this assessment with me?"

It might surprise you, but very few people knew what they wanted to achieve in the gym. Most of them would stare at me with a blank look on their face and say something like, "I want to get in better shape." Or, "I want to get into the routine of working out."

From a trainer's perspective, you have to realize this basically means nothing to me. Obviously they want to get in "better shape" or else they wouldn't be in the gym. So I would ask them, "What does getting in better shape mean to you? How would you define being in better shape?"

They would think for a minute, and then answer, "Well, I'd like to lose some weight I guess. I'd like to get stronger, too."

Now we're getting somewhere, but still, I need to know more. I want to know exactly what I should be designing their program to accomplish. So I would continue to press them, "Okay cool. So why do you want to lose weight? What would losing weight allow you to do?"

Again, they would stop and think. Some would laugh nervously, I was making them uncomfortable. But that was the whole point. I needed to get inside their head and understand their true motivation so I could know exactly who I was dealing with.

Eventually, they would reply, "I guess losing weight would allow me to look better and feel better about myself."

I pressed on, "Yeah that makes sense. But why exactly would it allow you to feel better?"

Here's where things get interesting. Some would say, "If I lose about 20 pounds then I could fit into my old jeans from 10 years ago. That would make me feel so youthful and full of energy."

Others would say, "I'm about to have a baby and I'm

afraid I won't be able to pick it up and play with it if I don't lose weight and get stronger."

Boom! That's what I was looking for.

You see, if they just wanted to lose weight because their spouse or friend told them they should, then they aren't going to be very motivated to show up and put in the work. Trust me, I took on many clients like this, only to see them quit after a couple weeks of training.

But if they want to lose weight so they can feel like they're 25 again, or so they can be a good parent for their future child, then they're going to be fired up and ready to crush every single workout.

They have "skin in the game" and they're intrinsically motivated to achieve their goal.

This means they're going to be a good client who will stick around for a while and see some awesome results. And these are the type of people I want to help out. Not only that, but it also makes it a whole lot easier for me to choose the most effective exercises for them.

For example, if they wanted to feel young again, then I would coach them like they were an athlete training to compete. Or if they wanted to be able to play with their future kid, then I would have them pick things up off the floor to simulate playing with a child.

By understanding their motivations – and getting them to be acutely aware of them – it clarifies whether or not they should be pursuing this goal in the first place. It also clarifies the exact steps they should take in order to be successful.

And this applies to more than just fitness and personal training. In fact, it applies to literally everything you pursue in life.

Mindset #16: Understanding my motivations will clarify my direction in life.

You need to stop blindly pursuing things in life.

You must make this mindset shift – and understand your true motivations – in order to stop living life unconsciously.

It will allow you to make faster progress and see better results in the areas of your life that are actually important to you. It will allow you to stop wasting your time pursuing things that don't really matter to you. And it will clarify what goals are worth pursuing in the future.

This is not just some BS theory of mine. Lots of research has been done to back it up.

One study was conducted on 1,042 students at the University of Quebec in Canada. All of these students were enrolled in the same class at the beginning of the year. And they all completed an assessment to determine their motivation for taking the course.

At the end of the semester, researchers found that students who were intrinsically motivated to take the course were far more likely stay in the course and earn high marks versus those who took the course simply because they were required to or because they needed to earn credits. [19]

In other words, students who took the course because they were actually interested in the material were far less likely to drop out than students who were taking it to fulfill a requirement.

While this seems logical, it's still a bit surprising. Even if they were less interested in the course material, you would still expect the second group of students to stay in the course and get the credits they needed. But they didn't. And the ones who did got worse grades.

This proves that your motivations really matter. If you're intrinsically motivated to do something – meaning that you actually enjoy doing it – then you're far more likely to succeed than if you were just doing it to earn some external "reward". You're also more likely to do a better job.

Look, I could list more and more studies just like this one, but I don't want to bore you. Here are a few more examples to make things clear:

Employees who actually enjoy their work perform far more efficiently than employees who are only motivated by the prospect of getting a paycheck or avoiding getting fired. People who experience sickness or illness as a result of their bad habits are far more likely to quit than people who are only motivated to quit because someone told them they should. And, as we covered earlier, people who start working out to overcome a personal struggle are far more likely to lose weight and get in shape than people who just want to lose 20 pounds because they think that they "should". The list goes on and on...

The point I'm making is that by simply being aware of your motivations you can side-step a lot of issues in your life. You will realize what's worth pursuing and what's not actually important to you. You can start living up to your own values rather than just trying to please other people.

You will also become far more successful – in your career, your health, and your relationships – because of it.

So how do you decide what's worth pursuing and what you should give up on?

It all comes down to whether or not you actually want something, or whether you're just pursuing it for an external reward.

A simple way to determine your true motivations for doing something is to ask yourself why you're doing it. But don't stop there. You should ask yourself "why?" at least 3 or 4 times, because your first few answers are likely just scratching the surface.

For example, right now I'm training in Muay Thai (a martial art). So I would ask myself, "Why am I training in Muay Thai?"

Then I would answer, "Because I want to learn how to fight."

Then I would ask myself, "Why do I want to learn how to fight?"

Then I would answer, "Because I want to be able to defend myself."

Then I would ask myself, "Why do I want to be able to defend myself?"

Then I would answer, "Because it will make me feel stronger and more courageous."

Then I would ask myself, "Why do I want to feel stronger and more courageous?"

Then I would answer, "Because being strong and courageous are two important values for me."

I now know my deeper motivation for pursuing martial arts. This will give me the push I need to consistently train hard, improve my skills, and develop the strength and courage I seek.

If you are not able to keep coming up with an answer after the first or second "why" then you probably don't have a great motivation for that particular goal. And this means you should consider dropping it.

Challenge

What's the main thing holding you back you in life right now?

Bad things happen to all of us. It's an inevitable part of life.

Being able to accept these obstacles when they come up, and then move past them, is what separates happy, successful people from miserable, complacent people.

Your health is not going to be perfect. You're going to get sick, get injured, and probably even develop some chronic health conditions as you grow older.

Your relationships aren't going to be perfect. You're going to get angry at your partner, feel lonely, and probably even get cheated on once or twice.

Your career is not going to be perfect. You're going to have boring tasks to do, miss out on promotions, and probably even lose your job once or twice.

If you start your business, this isn't going to be perfect either. You're going to struggle to attract customers, struggle to grow your brand, and probably even lose money along the way.

You're going to face obstacles at every turn. This is the reality of life.

How you interpret these obstacles, and how you react to them, is what will determine if you can stay positive, get past them, and live a good life. Otherwise, you will succumb to anxiety, feel sorry for yourself, and fail to overcome your struggles.

Most people succumb to their obstacles. They allow themselves to be defeated. They assume the "victim" mentality. They cry, "Oh, poor me!" And they sit around and feel sorry for themselves.

If you focus only on your problems, then you're doomed to be miserable and fail.

Think about this: when you see a close friend or family member go through a tough breakup, lose their job, or get diagnosed with an unfortunate health condition, how do they usually react? Do they fight back and find a way to quickly recover and get on with their lives? Or do they act defeated and lose their will to live?

If you're like me, then I'm sure it's both frustrating and saddening when they act defeated. I'm sure you're quick to try and cheer them up. I'm sure you're quick to tell them to start moving forward, no matter how bleak and depressing their current situation is. I'm sure you advise them to stop talking to their ex, or to start applying for new jobs, or to just take their medication and focus on getting healthy.

Here's the thing: it's easy to see how other people should react to their circumstances in order to bounce back. But do you? When *you* go through a tough breakup, lose your job, or get diagnosed with an unfortunate health condition, how do you react? Do you move forward? Or do you dwell on the shitty circumstances?

I'm sure sometimes you bounce back faster than others. I'm sure sometimes you identify the best course of action and immediately get started working on it.

But I'm also sure that sometimes you get stuck in the trap of feeling sorry for yourself, and fail to do much except sit around and be miserable.

Mindset #17: Failure is feedback. Every obstacle I face is feedback I can use to move forward and grow stronger.

This mindset is the secret to bouncing back every time. This mindset is the key to refusing to let unforeseen obstacles derail your progress and knock you down.

I stole this mindset from the great Roman emperor

and philosopher, Marcus Aurelius. In his famous book *Meditations*, he writes:

"Our actions may be impeded, but there can be no impeding our intentions. Because we can accommodate and adapt... The impediment to action advances action. What stands in the way becomes the way."

Let's break that down, one sentence at a time.

"Our actions may be impeded, but there can be no impeding our intentions."

While certain obstacles can prevent you from carrying out your plan of action, they cannot prevent you from pursuing your ultimate goal.

For example, I self-published my first book because I wanted to share my knowledge with as many people as possible, and make some money in the process. However, when I released it, barely anyone bought it.

My action – selling my book to thousands of people – was impeded. But my intention – reaching thousands of people to share my knowledge – was not. Even though my first attempt failed, I still wanted to achieve the same outcome.

This happens to almost anyone who sets a goal. Your first attempt to start a business, get a girlfriend, or transform your body will almost always fail. But that does not stop you from wanting a successful business, a loving girlfriend, or a jacked body. No, of course not. Even though your actions were impeded, your intention remains the same.

"Because we can accommodate and adapt…"

Regardless of what happens, you always have the ability to persist and figure out a different way to attack the situation.

For example, after my first book failed, I still had the choice to remain resilient and adapt to the situation. I still wanted to spread my message to thousands of people and make some money in the process. I simply had to re-think my plan of action.

You too can remain resilient in the face of failure. Yes, something went wrong and your initial plan failed. But is that going to stop you from reaching your goal? Or are you going to persist and figure out a new way to make it work? The choice – and it *is* a choice that you get to make – is yours.

"The impediment to action advances action. What stands in the way becomes the way."

Here's the real magic. Here's where the real genius of Marcus Aurelius exposes itself.

Every obstacle that you face is telling you something. And it's not just telling you that you failed, or that you were wrong. No, it's giving you valuable feedback about what your next step should be. It's paving the way forward and helping you reach your desired outcome.

For example, after my first book failed, I saw two distinct choices. I could write another book or I could figure out a different way to spread my message. However, the small amount of people who bought my book left good reviews. They enjoyed it and encouraged me to write another.

So then it was clear to me. I would write another book, but this time around I would put more effort into "launching" the book and promoting it. After all, I knew I could write a good book, I just hadn't figured out how to sell it yet.

I took this feedback and started researching how to sell books on Amazon. Before long, I discovered a new launch strategy that I could use for my next book. And you know what? It worked. The next book sold like crazy, and I successfully achieved my goal of spreading my message to thousands of people and becoming an Amazon bestselling author.

Obviously, I'm glossing over lots of details, but the point is that "failure is feedback". Or as Marcus says, "What stands in the way becomes the way."

You too can adopt this mindset and use it to overcome obstacles in your own life. You too can view your failures as feedback. You can analyze them and use them to pave the path forward.

Not only does this make failures less painful, it also makes success inevitable. By allowing your obstacles to show you what your next step should be, you will always be able to bounce back and keep moving forward. Before you know it, you will reach your goal.

All you have to do is view your struggles as opportunities to grow stronger and move forward.

One more thing. If you're struggling to identify exactly what the current obstacle you're facing is telling you to do, realize that someone else has undoubtedly overcome this challenge in the past. All you have to do is find out what they did. And lucky for you, a quick internet search should yield the answer.

Progress

Do you make a lot of mistakes? Or do you avoid mistakes at all costs?

Back in Part 1, we discussed how trying to be perfect can cause you to be ashamed of your insecurities and sabotage your self-esteem.

But there's something else that trying to be perfect does: it paralyzes you.

If you're afraid of slipping up and making mistakes, then you're going to hesitate to take action. If you're afraid that things might go wrong, then you're more likely to avoid taking risks in life. And if you avoid taking risks, and you avoid making mistakes, then you're never going to achieve anything noteworthy.

Back when I was in high school, I made this mistake. I made the mistake of being afraid of making mistakes. All the way up until that point, I excelled as a basketball player. But when I got to high school, my new coach scared me. Every time I made a mistake, he yelled at me.

Rather than using this as motivation to play harder, I used it as motivation to try and avoid making any mistakes. Little by little, I stopped trying to dribble the ball if there was a defender nearby, because I didn't want to lose possession and let him steal it. I stopped trying to shoot the ball, because I didn't want to screw up and miss the shot. I even stopped trying to make too many passes, because I didn't want to give the other team the ball by accident.

Within a few weeks, I completely sucked. All of the skill and confidence I'd built up over my childhood years suddenly vanished. I was playing in a state of constant fear. I was afraid of screwing up. And that completely paralyzed me.

Rather than being the aggressive scorer I had been all my life, I could barely do anything. Even though I entered the season as perhaps the best player on the team, I might have been the worst by the end of the year...

And this didn't end on the basketball court. All of a sudden, I let this mindset seep into the rest of my life. Now, as guys were starting to ask girls out, I was afraid of making a mistake and getting rejected. I let this fear paralyze me. I avoided talking to girls at all costs.

This toxic mindset crippled my confidence for the next 8 or 9 years of my life. Rather than meeting new people, exploring new interests, and enjoying myself, I spent most of my college years trapped inside my head. And it was all because I was afraid to make mistakes.

I don't tell you this story to depress you or ask for your pity. This experience – and all the mental pain that ensued – ultimately strengthened me. It ultimately taught me the value of taking risks and making mistakes.

And that's probably the most important lesson I've ever learned.

Mindset #18: I'm not perfect, I'm a work in progress. Making mistakes is making progress.

Here's the harsh truth: there are many things you will never be 100% prepared for in life.

It doesn't matter if this means asking a girl out, asking for a raise, starting a business, or writing a book. You will face countless situations that involve a large degree of uncertainty.

If you're afraid to screw up, then you're less likely to take the risk. And if you don't take the risk, then you have no chance of making progress and being successful.

In sports, they say, "You have to shoot to score." Well, the same holds true in all other areas of your life.

You have to shift your mindset from, "What if I screw up?" to, "Even if I screw up, I'll still be making progress."

You need to stop viewing mistakes as failure. Sure, a mistake is a temporary failure. But it's also an inevitable part of success. As Michael Jordan – perhaps the most successful athlete of all time – once said:

"I've missed more than 9000 shots in my career. I've lost almost 300 games. 26 times, I've been trusted to take the game-winning shot and missed. I've failed over and over and over again in my life. And that is why I succeed."

There's no such thing as an overnight success. Every successful person you've heard of has made thousands, if not millions, of mistakes. It's their ability to tolerate these mistakes and keep going that makes them successful.

You have to realize that the only way to excel in life and achieve your goals is to look at yourself as a never-ending work in progress. You will never be perfect. You will never reach a point where your work is done. In order to grow and move forward, you must make mistakes.

Making mistakes is making progress.

And, as we explored in the previous chapter, making mistakes is what shows you the way forward. Without the guidance and feedback of your failures, you will never find the path to success.

Look, even if you make this mindset shift, you're still going to be afraid of making mistakes. It's human nature. The fear of making mistakes is never going to disappear. It's deeply ingrained into our subconscious minds. Our ancient ancestors needed this fear to keep them alive. For them, one mistake could have been the difference between life and death.

But times have changed. Today, mistakes and failures rarely have the chance to hurt you. So you must work to overcome this fear, and avoid the paralysis and stagnation it leads to.

You must adopt this mindset: "I am not perfect, I am a work in progress."

This might be the most empowering belief in this entire book. It acknowledges your limits and your imperfections, but it refuses to let them keep you down. It prepares you for the inevitable failures in your future. And it gives you the strength to keep going, regardless of how many times you screw up.

As Marcus Aurelius once said, "You have power over your mind – not outside events. Realize this, and you will find strength."

I hope that reading this book has helped you make this realization in your life. I hope that reading this book has allowed you to take control of your mindsets...

Because, at the end of the day, you only have power over your mind – not outside events.

.

The 18 Mindsets

Below you will find a list of all 18 mindsets covered in this book. Put them into action. Commit them to memory. And come back to this list whenever you need a reminder.

Part I: Self-Awareness

#1: My suffering is merely a test, it is merely a chance to practice my virtues.

#2: I am not perfect, but I love myself anyway.

#3: My emotions, my actions, and my decisions are my responsibility and nobody else's.

#4: Negative self-talk is normal, but engaging it only makes things worse.

#5: My time is my most valuable resource.

#6: The less there is to worry about, the more I can focus on what really matters, and the better I can perform.

Part II: Relationships

#7: Everybody is self-conscious.

#8: I genuinely want other people to be happy and successful.

#9: I am happier, more confident, and more attractive when I express myself unapologetically.

#10: I can learn something from everyone I talk to.

#11: Certain things should not be tolerated.

#12: Living up to my own values is more important than getting approval from other people.

Part III: Achievement

#13: Pursuing my interests will make me happier now, and it can also lead to game-changing opportunities in the future.

#14: My next mission is the most important one.

#15: All that matters is taking the next step, no matter how small it is.

#16: Understanding my motivations will clarify my direction in life.

#17: Failure is feedback. Every obstacle I face is feedback I can use to move forward and grow stronger.

#18: I'm not perfect, I'm a work in progress. Making mistakes is making progress.

Your Next Step

There's no doubt in my mind that you're well on your way to mastering your mindsets, transforming your self-confidence, and accomplishing bigger goals!

But here's the thing...

The mindsets and exercises in this book are only effective if you actually do them!

That's why I created a Confidence Hacks "Cheat Sheet" to help you get started.

Inside you'll learn 7 proven exercises to instantly boost your confidence, including:

- How to instantly appear more confident and attractive
- A simple affirmation to rapidly boost self-esteem
- A proven method to enhance your motivation and focus

...and much, much more.

Download it here:
http://www.howtobeast.com/get-confident

Can You Do Me a Favor?

Thanks for checking out my book.

I'm confident you will build a strong, healthy mindset if you follow what's written inside. But before you go, I have one small favor to ask...

Would you take 60 seconds and write a quick blurb about this book on Amazon?

Reviews are the best way for independent authors (like me) to get noticed, sell more books, and spread my message to as many people as possible. I also read every review and use the feedback to write future revisions – and future books, even.

Thank you – I really appreciate your support.

My Other Books

If you enjoyed this book, you'll definitely want to read my others. Check them out at this link:

www.howtobeast.com/my-books

About the Author

David de las Morenas is a bestselling author, certified strength coach, and the founder of **www.HowToBeast.com** – a popular website for men who want to build confidence, build muscle, and unleash their inner beast!

References

1. Haddon Klingberg (16 October 2001). When life calls out to us: the love and lifework of Viktor and Elly Frankl. Doubleday. ISBN 978-0-385-50036-4.

2. Bastiani, Andrea M., et al. "Perfectionism in anorexia nervosa." International Journal of Eating Disorders 17.2 (1995): 147-152.

3. Blatt, Sidney J. "The destructiveness of perfectionism: Implications for the treatment of depression." American psychologist 50.12 (1995): 1003.

4. Flett, Gordon L., Paul L. Hewitt, and Dennis G. Dyck. "Self-oriented perfectionism, neuroticism and anxiety." Personality and Individual Differences 10.7 (1989): 731-735.

5. Halvorson, Bengt. "2011 Honda Civic." The Car Connection. Internet Brands, Inc. Web. 02 Aug. 2016.

6. Rechtin, Mark. "Honda CEO Ito Takes Responsibility for Civic's U.S. Troubles." Automotive News. Crain Communications, Inc. Web. 02 Aug. 2016.

7. Wardlaw, Christian. "2013 Honda Civic: New vs. Old." Autotrader. Autotrader, Inc. Web. 02 Aug.

2016.

8. Cain, Timothy. "Honda Civic Sales Figures." Good Car Bad Car. Web. 02 Aug. 2016.

9. "Conquering a Video Game Addiction." Outside the Lines. ESPN Internet Ventures. Web. 02 Aug. 2016.

10. Mayer, Richard E., et al. "When less is more: Meaningful learning from visual and verbal summaries of science textbook lessons." Journal of educational psychology 88.1 (1996): 64.

11. Iyengar, Sheena S., and Mark R. Lepper. "When choice is demotivating: Can one desire too much of a good thing?." Journal of personality and social psychology 79.6 (2000): 995.

12. Nemeth, Charlan Jeanne. "Managing innovation: When less is more." California management review 40.1 (1997): 59-74.

13. Paffenbarger, Ralph S., I-M. Lee, and R. Leung. "Physical activity and personal characteristics associated with depression and suicide in American college men." Acta Psychiatrica Scandinavica 89.s377 (1994): 16-22.

14. Wegner, Brandy S., Anita M. Hartmann, and C. R. Geist. "Effect of exposure to photographs of thin models on self-consciousness in female college students." Psychological Reports (2000).

15. Dunn, Elizabeth W., Lara B. Aknin, and Michael I. Norton. "Spending money on others promotes happiness." Science 319.5870 (2008): 1687-1688.

16. Tamir, Diana I., and Jason P. Mitchell. "Disclosing information about the self is intrinsically rewarding." Proceedings of the National Academy of Sciences 109.21 (2012): 8038-8043.

17. MacDonald, Geoff, Jennifer L. Saltzman, and Mark R. Leary. "Social approval and trait self-esteem." Journal of Research in Personality 37.2 (2003): 23-40.

18. Harden, Seth. "New Years Resolution Statistics." Statistic Brain. Statistic Brain Research Institute. Web. 02 Aug. 2016.

19. Vallerand, Robert J., and Robert Blssonnette. "Intrinsic, extrinsic, and amotivational styles as predictors of behavior: A prospective study." Journal of personality 60.3 (1992): 599-620.

CPSIA information can be obtained
at www.ICGtesting.com
Printed in the USA
BVOW06s2003231217
503558BV00017B/921/P